AS A
ROARING
LION

Understanding and Defeating
Your Greatest Enemy

PAUL
SCHWANKE

First published in 2010 by Striving Together Publications, a
ministry of Lancaster Baptist Church, Lancaster, CA 93535.
Striving Together Publications is committed to providing
tried, trusted, and proven books that will further equip local
churches to carry out the Great Commission. Your comments
and suggestions are valued.

Striving Together Publications
4020 E. Lancaster Blvd.
Lancaster, CA 93535
800.201.7748

Cover design by Andrew Jones
Layout by Craig Parker
Edited by Cary Schmidt and Monica Bass
Special thanks to our proofreaders

ISBN 978-1-59894-106-7

Printed in the United States of America

"In a day when Christians are falling prey to the enemy left and right, *As a Roaring Lion* is a must-read for the believer who is striving to live on the victory side of the Christian life."

Pastor Dave Crichton

Lakeside Baptist Church

Peoria, Arizona

"Paul Schwanke is a seasoned veteran in the battle for Christian victory over our archenemy, Satan. In *As a Roaring Lion,* he artfully brings the spiritual canvass of our lives into full view as he provides perceptive insight into the most significant matters of the Christian experience. Brother Schwanke possesses an amazing analytical mind coupled with sensitivity and compassion. With balanced clarity, he passionately instills scriptural truths in the believer that will strengthen his faith, secure his heart, and stabilize his life. This is a book that should be in every Christian's home."

Pastor Bob Gass

Harvest Baptist Church

Medford, Oregon

"Evangelist Paul Schwanke has interwoven clear Bible teaching with heart-moving illustrations and real life experiences to unmask and expose Satan for who he is and what he does. *As a Roaring Lion* is a must-read for every growing Christian. I enthusiastically recommend it."

Pastor Doug Meader

Lakes Pond Baptist Church
Waterford, Connecticut

"In this book you will find the heart of an evangelist who has preached the Cross, the blood, the Bible, and has fought the evil one for over twenty-five years. I recommend *As a Roaring Lion.*"

Pastor Dennis Walker

Open Door Baptist Church
Summit, Mississippi

CONTENTS

ACKNOWLEDGMENTS

One of the greatest privileges of living the life of an evangelist is the honor of spending quality time with some of the finest independent Baptist pastors around the world. From each one, I am able to glean insight into both the Word and work of God. I am especially grateful for Pastor Dennis Walker of the Open Door Baptist Church of Summit, Mississippi for his encouragement in writing this book.

I also am thankful to my son Tim who has been serving our country in the U.S. Army since 2005. Your descriptions of a soldier fighting a physical battle have been a real help in understanding our spiritual battle. I realize that I am able to preach nightly without fear of men because of the dedication of those in our U.S. military protecting our freedom. Thanks as well to my daughter-in-law Katie, who like multitudes of military wives and family members, bear the burden of lonely nights and anxious days supporting those on the front lines.

I wish to extend my gratitude as well to Pastor Paul Chappell, Assistant Pastor Cary Schmidt, and the tremendous staff at Lancaster Baptist Church and Striving Together Publications for their patience and help in publishing this book. Thanks for giving an opportunity to a raw rookie like me!

But most of all, "…thanks be unto God, which always causeth us to triumph in Christ…" (2 Corinthians 2:14). At times, our battle with the enemy seems almost hopeless, our struggle insurmountable, yet, as an old preacher put it, "We are not even on the winning side. We are on the side that already won!"

INTRODUCTION

When I first entered the ministry of local church evangelism in 1983, I chose 1 Corinthians 1:18 as a theme verse. "For the preaching of the cross is to them that perish foolishness; but unto us which are saved it is the power of God." I fell in love with the entire chapter and am still today amazed that God would choose a method (preaching) that in the eyes of the world was foolish, but in the wisdom of Heaven was full of "power." I delight in the fact that God in His infinite brilliance would choose a simple, plain message of "Christ crucified" (1 Corinthians 1:23) to pull even the vilest of sinners out of a miry pit. He is not fazed by the scoffing intellectuals that ridicule the blood and go so far as to call it "foolish."

I am especially thankful that God is willing to use individuals that the lost world regards as "foolish...weak...base...[and] despised" (1 Corinthians 1:27–28). I have learned that God doesn't need the majority, and He doesn't need a consensus. He is looking for one. One man. One teenager. One church. One family.

When the world was overwhelmed by wickedness, one man, Noah, found grace. When the prophets of Baal were in the thousands, one man, Elijah, took his stand. From Abel to Zachariah, from John the Baptist to Pastor John, God has reminded us again and again that all it takes is one righteous man. No one is unimportant to God. No casualty in the family of God is an acceptable loss. God uses "one man."

Satan has a similar strategy. If he can destroy one man he can destroy a family. If he can destroy one family he can destroy a church. If he can destroy one church he can destroy a nation. Humans, in the presence of disaster, have a tendency to seek for grand conspiracy theories, yet a careful look at most human tragedies would see a failure of "one man."

Often, we look at the battlefield as a whole. We see the large issues and the general problems. We are correctly alarmed by the statistics and movements that increasingly forsake the Bible. It is important to see the big picture, but while we view the army as a whole, we must never neglect the single soldier. Satan desires to sift them one by one, and that includes you and me.

Hence, God has placed a somber warning in the Bible. It is a wake-up call for every child of God.

"Be sober, be vigilant; because your adversary the devil, as a roaring lion, walketh about, seeking whom he may devour" (1 Peter 5:8).

CHAPTER ONE

AN ENEMY IS AFTER YOU

ed Daub has given his life to be a church planter in the land of Kenya, East Africa. As a young evangelist, it was my privilege to preach a series of meetings with him and gain a vastly expanded perspective of the ministry. The incredible atmosphere experienced when a preacher walks into a mud hut absolutely packed with African saints singing with all their might is an immense contradiction from the compromised, canned "worship" that the Hollywood culture has inflicted upon American churches. Standing in a public school assembly and freely preaching Christ crucified to 1,200 teenagers is more than we could "ask or think" (Ephesians 3:20). The fellowship with young men who had dedicated their lives for the "preaching of the cross"

(1 Corinthians 1:18) became a powerful conviction to my own life with its reminder that some still have to count the cost to follow Christ. What a glorious time!

There was one problem—Ted's library.

Browsing through his library after one of the evening services, I came across a fascinating book called, *Death in the Long Grass*, written by safari hunter Peter Capstick. He told of man-eating leopards prowling the jungle paths and deadly mambas slashing at their victims. There were stories of hippos and cape buffaloes mowing down everybody in their path, and of elephants grinding people into the dirt. Of course, there were the lions. Tales of these mighty cats stalking their prey through the long grass riveted my attention. From crocodiles to rhinos to hyenas to lions, the life and death accounts in the book made it impossible to lay aside.[1]

"Bwana" Daub, the fearless missionary, had set aside a day to explore the Samburu National Reserve, a fabulous park full of elephants, monkeys, rhinos, cape buffaloes, and more elephants. Ted is a wonderful Christian with this one nasty habit. He loves to honk the horn of his van and torment elephants until they are ready to charge. Then, with his wife and daughters screaming, he slams the stick in reverse and drives for his life.

I should have seen it coming. Late one night, we were driving on an African "highway" at some 100 kph (62 mph) when I saw shadows ahead on the dark road. As Ted responded to my pleadings by locking up the brakes, we came within inches of a family of giraffes crossing the road. Had we gone a little farther, a ton and a half of giraffe meat would have sent us out into eternity. How noble would that be? The Apostle John died in boiling oil, Daniel faced the roaring lions, Peter was crucified upside down, and I almost died by giraffe.

We had spent a wonderful day enjoying the beautiful African creation, laughing at the mischievous monkeys, witnessing more species of deer than I ever dreamed existed, and running for our lives from elephants. And then it happened—with a loud "BAM," we had a flat tire. Being a good missionary, Ted stepped out of the car to change the tire. Being a good evangelist, I stepped out of the car to watch Ted change the tire, and that is when I looked around.

Long grass. Everywhere—long grass.

I could almost feel the hot breath of some starving lion drooling over Baptist meat. I was convinced his eyes were squinting in the afternoon sun with that evil eye the king of the jungle gives as he is about ready to impose his rule on his kingdom. We had escaped the wrath of the elephants, I had eaten African chickens and lived to tell about it, I even survived the giraffe ordeal, and this was how it was going to end. At least death by lion sounds better than death by giraffe. (Capstick didn't even have a chapter on giraffes.)

> EVERY CHRISTIAN IS STALKED BY AN ENEMY MORE POWERFUL AND MENACING THAN A HUNGRY, AFRICAN LION.

It was then I felt a powerful urge to pray. I told Ted I would step in the vehicle and pray God's blessing on the tire change, and the veteran, pioneer missionary had to go it alone. And yes, Ted is still with us.

Every Christian is stalked by an enemy more powerful and menacing than a hungry, African lion. This enemy is lurking in the tall grass, and we have been warned.

"…your adversary the devil, as a roaring lion, walketh about, seeking whom he may devour" (1 Peter 5:8). One powerfully loaded verse shines the light of truth on our enemy.

Satan is our adversary, a word defined as an "opponent in a lawsuit."[2] There has never been a money grabbing lawyer who could twist words and phrases like this pernicious pettifogger from perdition.

He is at his worst in Job 1, as the Creator declares once and for eternity the character and testimony of Job. Job was "perfect and upright," he "feared God," and he "eschewed evil" (Job 1:1). A four-fold testimony has been entered into the eternal record book and is forever "settled in Heaven" (Psalm 119:89). He was so consistent, that his Heavenly Father could ask of Satan, "…Hast thou considered my servant Job, that there is none like him in the earth…" (Job 1:8). What an affirmation! Job, a man of integrity and righteousness, who feared God, turns his back on the slightest hint of wickedness!

Now watch the enemy paint that sly, shifty smile on his face. "You say that Job fears God? Well, look what you have done for him! You have put a hedge about him on every side and I cannot even get to him. You have given to him 'pressed down, and shaken together, and running over' (Luke 6:38), and the whole land sees his abounding substance. He does not serve you for nothing! Look what you have given him! You say that Job fears God? Well now, I guess that would all depend on what your definition of fear is!"

Exposed! Satan is the "accuser of our brethren" (Revelation 12:10). He stands before God day and night in the eternal courtroom of glory as the

> SATAN NEVER TIRES;
> HE NEVER GETS
> DISCOURAGED; AND
> HE NEVER QUITS.

plaintiff in the trial. He never tires; he never gets discouraged; and he never quits. He constantly bombards the Throne, tattling on the children of God.

How we must break the heart of our Father as He endures yet another litany of our sins. How Heaven must be flushed with embarrassment when the sordid details of secret transgressions are broadcast at the bar. If we could only see the pain, and experience the disgrace and dishonor our wickedness has created, we would cry with David, "…Blot out all mine iniquities. Create in me a clean heart…" (Psalm 51:9–10).

First Peter 5:8 also exposes Satan's strategy—he wants to be on offense. He "walketh about" and actively seeks the vulnerable Christian "whom he may devour." Heaven does not apologize for truth, and the morbid fact stands. There is a vicious enemy prowling in our homes and churches who will not be satisfied until he can plunge his diabolical fangs into our lives, our homes, our marriages, and our churches. He refuses to shake the victim loose until he has extracted a bloody victory.

The unique terror of a ravaging lion causes an unrivaled fear that trembles the human soul. Ask the citizens of Njombe, Tanzania. From 1932–1947, a pride of marauding lions terrorized their village resulting in the gruesome deaths of one thousand villagers.[3] Ask the noted missionary David Livingston. Like the Apostle Paul, he was "delivered out of the mouth of the lion" (2 Timothy 4:17), and his crushed shoulder would daily remind him of that encounter until he graduated to glory. The lion of the jungle is vastly different from the Disney Lion King.

Multitudes of Christians donate an hour of their time to "Disney Channel" religion. The Sunday morning entertainment hour, complete with a safari guide who refuses to alert the church member of the enemy prowling in the long grass, has produced a generation of fattened wildebeests that are easy prey. For all of the surveys and statistics, the conferences and conventions, the meetings and methods, and the experts and expertise, the sad state of affairs could not be more evident.

God's Word warns us, "Be sober!" "Be vigilant!" Wake up and watch out! The enemy is laying low in the long grass biding his time. He wants you.

CHAPTER TWO

KNOW YOUR ENEMY

The New England Patriots created quite a stir in 2007. Speculation erupted in sports pages across America when the team's illegal filming of opponents' workouts was disclosed. Questions were raised about a past Super Bowl victory over the St. Louis Rams, and the merits of their near perfect season were brought into question. "Spygate" ultimately found itself in the Halls of the United States Senate with Senator Arlen Specter accusing the Patriots of "stonewalling" the investigation.[1]

If nothing else, Patriot Coach Brian Belichick knows the importance of scouting the enemy.

Marge Schott was the long-time owner of the Cincinnati Reds. A once proud baseball program which stood at the pinnacle of the

9

baseball world in the 1970s had long since fallen to the lower tier of National League teams. The "Big Red Machine" had become the "Little Pink Tinker Toy" because, as the esteemed preacher Lee Roberson stated so often, "Everything rises and falls on leadership."

Marge Schott was famous for her uncanny ability to say the wrong thing at the wrong time. On one occasion, team personnel wanted to convince the gracious Mrs. Schott to increase the scouting budget in order to allow the Reds to not only scout their rivals, but also to discover better high school and college athletes. She refused the silly request noting, "Why do we pay these scouts at all? All they ever do is watch baseball games!"[2]

Mrs. Schott did not appreciate the importance of scouting the enemy.

Matthew 4 gives the godly man the scouting report of the ages. No secret cameras, no "overpaid" scouts, but rather, the King of kings and Lord of lords unmasks the roaring lion for all to see. Exposed is the enemy's character, his plan of attack, and his *modus operandi*. Most importantly, this scouting report gives the absolute, 100% guaranteed method whereby the child of God—be it a new baby in Christ or a seasoned saint in the family—can without question or reservation claim the victory. What simplicity yet what profundity! We follow this plan, and we win every time.

The public ministry of Jesus begins in Matthew 4:1 with an expression of His limitless love for helpless sinners. The One who flung the sun and the moon and the stars into space, the One who formed man out of the "dust of the ground," the One who breathed into his nostrils the "breath of life" (Genesis 2:7), was willing to submit Himself to the will of the Father. With full understanding of the battle that lay ahead, He was "…led up of the Spirit into the wilderness to be tempted of the devil."

Mark 1 emphasizes the incredible contrast taking place in that Judean wilderness. As Jesus submits to the waters of baptism, the heavens open and the Spirit of God descends upon Him. The skies boom as the mighty voice of God declares for all men and all time, "…Thou art my beloved Son, in whom I am well pleased" (Mark 1:11).

The refined scenery of the peaceful Jordan was about to change, for the Spirit immediately drove Him to the wilderness. Jesus trades the smooth waters for the rough terrain of a desolate wilderness. His confidants are no longer the disciples to be, but wild beasts. The first century creatures that inhabited the wild haunts of Judea were many, including boars and jackals and wolves and foxes and leopards and hyenas.[3] And of course, lions lived there, yet His greatest battle would not be with the king of the beasts, but rather, with the "prince of the power of the air" (Ephesians 2:2).

> THE KING OF KINGS AND LORD OF LORDS UNMASKS THE ROARING LION FOR ALL TO SEE.

The attacks are relentless. He is physically weakened from forty days of fasting. He is mentally weakened from the constant assaults of Satan. He is emotionally drained from the loneliness and the haunting screams of the night. Picture the forces of evil as they prepare for their final assault against Him. The marching demons have fortified themselves, pouring out their wrath and venom on one target. He has valiantly withstood the relentless assaults, but now all the ammunition that Hell can muster is pointed at its target. The evil serpent knows, "If I can cause Him to sin, I have won the battle of the ages."

This is the magnificent thing. He couldn't sin. He absolutely, positively was incapable of sinning. First John 3:5 says it all. "…in him is no sin." He could say to His foes, "Which of you convinceth me of sin…" (John 8:46) The judge who condemned Him to die had to say, "…I find no fault in this man" (Luke 23:4). The centurion who drove the nails testified, "…Certainly, this was a righteous man" (Luke 23:47). He knew no sin. He was separate from sinners. He was without sin, and there wasn't even a spot of subtle guile in Him. So then, what took Him to the wilderness to suffer such agony and horror?

He loves His children.

The torment, the isolation, the abuse of the Judean wasteland was a testimony of His desire for His children to be equipped to go to battle, and then win that battle against Satan. He submitted to the will of His Father so that He could not only leave a powerful example, but also have the ability to "…succor them that are tempted" (Hebrews 2:18). As foot-soldiers in His army, we make a deadly error when we trust in the arm of our own flesh in the battle against Satan. God has given us an eleven-verse battle plan for victory.

THE ENEMY DESCRIBED

Matthew 4 gives a brief but concise portrayal of the enemy. In verse 1 he is called the "devil." The word *devil* defines Satan as a slanderer, a false accuser, and an aggressor. He is always on offense. He is always probing and looking for weakness.

In verse 3, he is called the "tempter," meaning he is constantly questioning and casting doubt. He and his cohorts are in the business of raising question marks over the absolute truths of the Bible. His false "ministers of righteousness" (2 Corinthians 11:15) stand in seminary classrooms and compromised pulpits creating doubt in the minds of unsuspecting listeners. The first time he speaks in

> WE MAKE A DEADLY ERROR WHEN WE TRUST IN THE ARM OF OUR OWN FLESH IN THE BATTLE AGAINST SATAN.

the Old Testament, he says, "…Yea, hath God said…" (Genesis 3:1). The first time he speaks in the New Testament, he says, "…If thou be…" (Matthew 4:3). Satan's business is to perpetually cross-examine and contradict the words of God.

Matthew 4:3 also exposes him as a liar. His statement, "If thou be the Son of God," is a direct contradiction to the declaration of Almighty God. The voice thundered from Heaven in Matthew 3:17 as the Father set the record straight for time and eternity. He did not state, "This is one of my beloved sons." He did not state, "This is one of my created beings." The words could not be more forceful and direct. "This is my beloved Son, in whom I am well pleased."

Case closed. End of discussion. There is no need for interpreters or higher critics. The omnipotent, omniscient, King of Glory has declared it straight and true, yet that is not enough for Satan. He still finds a way to interrogate the clear, direct declaration of God. No wonder Jesus said, "...When he speaketh a lie, he speaketh of his own: for he is a liar, and the father of it" (John 8:44).

> SATAN'S BUSINESS IS TO PERPETUALLY CROSS-EXAMINE AND CONTRADICT THE WORDS OF GOD.

Verse 6 portrays the devil as crafty. It is so subtle and so devious that it might be easy to miss. With great pomp, he twists and misquotes Psalm 91:11–12 by removing a short phrase. Listen to Matthew 4:6, as he sounds so ministerial and spiritual in stating, "...it is written, He shall give his angels charge concerning thee." But Psalm 91:11 includes some words that Satan conveniently avoids, a phrase that says, "For he shall give his angels charge over thee, to keep thee **in all thy ways**." Those four words change the entire meaning of the verse. God's angels protect those who are living in obedience to the will of God, not the individual who follows the dictates of the devil.

A verse here, a phrase there, a passage here, a chapter there, and Satan's slick assaults on the Bible are hardly noticed. Even today his false prophets and teachers follow their master's plan with "…pernicious ways…covetousness…[and] feigned words [to] make merchandise" (2 Peter 2:2–3) of unsuspecting people. Ministers who ought to know better convince themselves and their listeners that as long as most of the Bible versions agree on most points of doctrine, what difference does it make? A well known radio talk show host states regularly, "Words mean things." When it comes to the Bible, the veracity of each verse, word, jot, and tittle are absolutely paramount.

The devil is also incredibly arrogant. It is the epitome of pretension to watch Satan join himself to Christ on the pinnacle of a great mountain in verse 8. As he shows Him the kingdoms of the world and their glory, he says, "…All these things will I give thee…" (Matthew 4:9). Please! Jesus spoke that very mountain into existence. Glory? One day He will come in power and great glory as the lightening flashing across the evening sky. Kingdoms? Excuse me. "…The kingdoms of this world are become the kingdoms of our Lord, and of his Christ; and he shall reign forever and ever" (Revelation 11:15).

The Enemy Debunked

The battle is engaged, and the Saviour exposes Satan's strategy. It is a three-pronged attack outlined in 1 John 2:16 as "the lust of the flesh, and the lust of the eyes, and the pride of life." He begins with "the lust of the flesh," tempting the Saviour to turn the stones into bread. Certainly, a Creator who speaks heavens into existence would have no difficulty in making a little stone edible. As Jesus was human, His hunger would be as of any person fasting forty days. Every fiber of His body would be crying for nourishment.

A long fast must be broken slowly with juices and water, and it has been suggested that Satan may have been trying to murder Him.[4] Unquestionably, the enemy desired Christ to reject His Father's will and submit Himself to Satan's will. It was a choice of being "led up of the spirit" or succumbing to Satan, a choice Jesus saw clearly.

The evil one has long corrupted the healthy, physical desires God has instilled in His creation. The beauty of sexual relations has been sabotaged by the Hollywood culture. The appetite for food can soon control a man to the point where the Bible warns of those whose "God is their belly" (Philippians 3:19). Any element of our lives that stifles our desire to do God's will can quickly place the wrong king on the throne of our lives.

Now watch the wicked one bring Jesus to a pinnacle rising 150 feet above the temple. With the Kidron Valley some 700 feet below, he opines, "Things are not working out for you. Your family members reject you. Your only converts are a handful of the lowest forms of humanity. The religious hierarchy does not respect you. It is time to make a splash. If you will cast yourself off, you will be the talk of the town."

This "pride of life" is a cancer that has claimed untold numbers of individual Christians, marriages, homes, and churches. How easy it becomes to convince ourselves that "we deserve better," "no one understands," "I haven't done anything wrong," "no one respects me," and "everybody is against me." Instead of rushing to the prayer closet, Christians are sitting on psychiatrists' couches. They seem to believe that the wisdom of daytime television is more desirable than the "wisdom that is from above" (James 3:17). Prescriptions have turned America into a nation of legal drug addicts, and even the United Nations claims that the "misuse of legal prescriptions surpasses the world-wide trade of illegal drugs."[5] "Jesus is all I need" has been replaced with "a pill is all I need."

> ANY ELEMENT OF OUR LIVES THAT STIFLES OUR DESIRE TO DO GOD'S WILL CAN QUICKLY PLACE THE WRONG KING ON THE THRONE OF OUR LIVES.

Unknown numbers of Christian couples can blame the "pride of life" for the downfall of their marriages. When a lost man is angry with his wife, the neighbors can hear the screaming and cursing. With the threats still bouncing off the walls, he furiously flees the house slamming the door behind him, and heads to the local liquor hall. But many Christians engage in a different sort of disagreement. No screaming, no violence, no tantrum, no drunkenness—it's a little more subtle. She will sit in one room watching her TV, and he will sit in another watching his. Stubborn pride keeps people from being right with each other.

Occasionally, the news stations will run a story of a church that has been destroyed by a backslidden preacher. Perhaps it is an affair, a money issue, or another wile of the evil one, but it is a sad day when dirty sins are made public. Everyone has heard those stories, yet, for every church ruined by the dirt of immorality, there have been countless churches ransacked by the pride of pastors and church members alike.

How many church business meetings feature infantile Christians like those described in 1 Corinthians 1 and 3? How many "Corinthian" believers poison their assemblies with the hypocritical claims of "super-spirituality?" "I am of Paul," "I am of Apollos," "I am of Cephas" come the fraudulent feigns of the phonies. Of course, the "peerless" Christians would smugly say, "I am of Christ." They certainly did not fool the Apostle Paul. "Ye are yet carnal: for whereas there is among you envying, and strife, and divisions, are ye not carnal, and walk as men?" He went so far as to tell them they were "babes."

Is it possible that present day churches are infected with the disease of Diotrephes? In 3 John 9–10, Diotrephes was identified as the church member "who loveth to have the preeminence among them." How sad is that testimony. Not "he loveth to encourage the brethren," not "he loveth to give to missions," not "he loveth to support his pastor," not "he loveth to give the Gospel to sinners," but he had to always be first. The noted evangelist Billy Sunday said the work of God might actually get somewhere if pastors did not have to spend so much time changing dirty diapers.

With his first two onslaughts against Christ safely spurned, Satan reaches into the quiver and pulls out arrow number three— "the lust of the eyes." From the exceeding high mountain, he makes his pitch. Knowing Christ to be the "Lamb slain from the foundation of the world" (Revelation 13:8), he tells him, "I can give you the kingdoms of the world without the death of Calvary. Kingdoms without a cross! No suffering! No Isaiah 53 for you! Everything you see with your eyes will be yours if you come my way."

That subtle, satanic attack still claims its victims. Many a child of the King has found himself gazing at the kingdoms and treasures of this world. The allure is powerful. "You don't have to die daily. You don't have to pick up your cross and follow Him. For me to live is Christ? I have an offer for you."

In the 1930s America was still in the throes of the Great Depression. A twenty-two-year-old insurance clerk with a deep, melodious voice was given the opportunity of a lifetime. A contract lay before him from a radio station that would make him a singing star, perhaps the "American Idol" of his day. A visit home to Canada found him sitting by his mother's piano, where she had quietly placed the words of a poem that providentially caught the eye of the star in waiting. As he read, his fingers subconsciously began to play across the piano keys. Soon, a melody had developed, but even more importantly, a choice had been made.

The young man by the piano was George Beverly Shea, and the words that seized his heart went like this:

> I'd rather have Jesus than silver or gold, I'd rather be His
>> than have riches untold;
> I'd rather have Jesus than houses or lands; I'd rather be
>> led by His nail-pierced hand.
> Than to be the king of a vast domain, or be held in sin's
>> dread sway;
> I'd rather have Jesus than anything this world
>> affords today.[6]

The Enemy Defeated

The critical lesson of Matthew 4 is the defeat of Satan. Every babe in Christ knows the importance of the Bible in gaining victory. We have memorized "Thy word have I hid in mine heart, that I might not sin against thee" (Psalm 119:11). Many Christian teenagers at one time or another have written in their Bibles, "This book will keep me from sin, or sin will keep me from this book." When Ephesians 6 is preached, we are reminded to wear the helmet of salvation, to wrap ourselves in righteousness and truth, to prepare our steps in proclaiming the gospel of peace, and to lift the shield of unshakeable faith. Then we are told we must wield the sword of the Spirit, "which is the word of God" (Ephesians 6:17). That is our weapon!

My son Tim defends America as a soldier in the Tenth Mountain Division. As this chapter is written, he is on his second tour of duty battling terrorism in the hotbed of Iraq. When Tim completed boot camp, I asked him the lesson that impressed him most. He told me he was taught to "keep his weapon close." At any moment and from any place, the enemy can strike. There is never an excuse for a soldier to be apart from his weapon which must always be clean and ready. A soldier who is casual with his gun is liable to become a casualty.

This principle is true for the Christian as well. As the armor of God is dispensed, we are given only one means of offense. The helmet, the breastplate, the belt, the shoes, and the shield are all defensive, but the sword is our only means of attack. Keep your sword close. Keep your sword ready. Keep your sword sharpened. We never know when the next battle

KEEP YOUR SWORD CLOSE.

will begin. We cannot tell when the next temptation will strike. We are never warned when the lion is crouching in the tall grass and ready to attack.

Matthew 4 gives an astounding lesson in using the Bible to defeat the enemy. As the military historian loves to study the strategies of Alexander the Great, Napoleon, Winston Churchill, or Douglas MacArthur, so the child of God must master the methods of the Saviour. When the enemy strikes, the Lord Jesus Christ, the living Word of God, teaches us to place paramount importance on availing ourselves of the written Word of God. Watch the Saviour brandish the Bible to claim victory.

Jesus had a complete and unshakeable confidence in the Bible. In Matthew 4:4, 7, and 10 He uses the same phrase, "It is written." That phrase was actually one word in the Greek language: *Gegraptai.* The ancient Greeks would engrave pictures and letters into stone or wood, and then tie two of the tablets together.[7] In a real way their letters and stories would be "written in stone." As Moses carried the law inscribed in stone by the hand of God, and as great monuments inscribe the words of great men to be remembered through the ages, so Jesus believed that the words of the Bible were inscribed and unchangeable.

GOD'S WORD STANDS TODAY AS IT WAS WRITTEN THEN.

Jesus believed something else about the Bible. Notice, He did not say, "It *was* written." Modern day scholars who scoff at a preserved Bible tell us the Bible is only perfect in its original autographs. Jesus did not accept that idea. The phrase "it is written" is a statement of the "indisputable and legal authority" of the Bible.[8] In effect, Jesus was saying, "It was written and inscribed accurately; and today, I have the Bible as it was written then." No wonder He could stand in the synagogue of Nazareth, read from the book of Isaiah, and then say, "…This day is this Scripture fulfilled in your ears" (Luke 4:21).

What power that confidence gives a child of God! What power that confidence lends to a Bible preacher. That power caused the arresting officers to say, "…Never man spake like this man" (John 7:46). That power created an astonishment in the multitude because "he taught them as one having authority, and not as the scribes" (Matthew 7:29). That same power would one day allow Peter and John to preach and testify with such boldness that the religious enemies would have to marvel and admit, "…they had been with Jesus" (Acts 4:13). That power separates the God-called Bible preacher from the morass of seminary-ordained ministers who preach without conviction and urgency. We preach the Bible because "It is written." It stands today as it was written then.

If the rocks and mountains of the Judean wilderness were called to testify of the events that took place centuries ago, they would ring out that one powerful testimony from the lips of the King. One simple phrase. One simple truth. "It is written." We don't add to it; we don't remove from it. It stands today as it stood then. "It is written." Case closed.

Keep your weapon close.

Jesus also demonstrated a competency in handling the Bible. Had the typical Christian gone to battle in Matthew 4, the responses would have been quite different. "I know there is a verse somewhere. Let me find my Bible concordance and look it up." "You will have to wait while I boot up my computer and then start my Bible program and I will search for the verse." "I will call my pastor and he will tell me what to do." "Let me go buy the latest book by the Christian psychiatrist and find an appropriate chart."

When Satan attacked, Jesus was ready. Assault number one was met by quoting Deuteronomy 8:3. Assault number two was handled by quoting Deuteronomy 6:16. Assault number three met its match at Deuteronomy 6:13. Three attacks were defeated by three verses Jesus had memorized. If the Living Word of God felt it necessary to memorize the written Word of God, then His saints should be on a Bible memory program. It must be decided that "…This book of the law shall not depart out of thy mouth…" and we will "…meditate therein day and night…" (Joshua 1:8). We build our Christian lives by reading the Bible, studying the Bible, meditating on the Bible, and hiding it in our hearts.

> WHEN SATAN ATTACKED, JESUS WAS READY.

Keep your weapon close.

It is noted as well that Jesus exhibited a consistency with the Bible. Matthew 4 records only three attempted ambushes, yet Luke 4:2 indicates there were forty days of attacks. Had all of the assaults been chronicled, we would be assured that every time the enemy tried to tempt Him, He responded with the Bible. Plan

"A" is to go to the Bible. There is no plan "B." The Bible works the first time, the last time, and every time. When we rely on our old trustworthy sword, we are on victorious ground. When "thus saith the Lord" is replaced with "thus saith the scholar" then "look out below." Great is the fall of the Christian who promotes his own reasoning over the Word of God.

All conquering Christians recognize the Bible as the prime foundation for a life equipped to battle the foe. For all of the modern philosophies, attitudes, programs, and analysis, the only way for the child of God to rise above the enemy is to return to the basics—return to the Bible.

There must be a daily habit of reading God's Word. Before a man heads to work, it is critical to spend the first few moments of a day in the Bible. This is a good time to use a Bible reading plan, perhaps finishing the Bible in a year. If a man has a lengthy commute, the Bible on CD beats the latest 'breaking news' on the radio.

STRONG CHRISTIAN LIVES ARE NOT BUILT IN A DAY.

There must also be times of Bible study. Pick a book of the Bible and slow things down. Instead of reading chapters, break the verses down into small portions grasping a deeper understanding of the Word of God. A good Bible dictionary and a good Bible concordance will enhance your understanding of particular Bible words. It might be wise to ask your pastor to recommend a commentary (a book about the Bible written by a man) never forgetting that the Bible is perfect and the commentary is not. One of the best methods of digesting the Bible is to ask simple questions. Who is this written to? Who is the author God is giving His words to? What are the issues of the day the recipient is dealing with? What other Scriptures expound on this text?

There must be a *consistent* Bible memory program. This can be done while taking a walk, running on a treadmill, relaxing during a coffee break, or, for many husbands, while waiting in the Wal-Mart parking lot for your wife. Begin by memorizing the Bible topically. Your pastor can recommend a good Bible memory program. Later, try to memorize an entire book of the Bible.

Set aside time to build a "family altar." Again the key is consistency. Find a few minutes when your family can gather together (perhaps after a meal or when the children are ready for bed). Read a few verses of the Bible, pray, sing a chorus, and then memorize the Bible as a family. An effective family altar only needs ten minutes a day, but it will solidify the Word of God in your home as nothing else.

Determine to be faithful to the local church. Sunday school, Sunday morning, Sunday evening, midweek service, revival meetings, prayer meetings, missions conferences, Bible conferences, family camps, and any other preaching services are golden opportunities to feast at the table of God's Word. Take your whole family and take your Bible.

Many question where to begin when studying the Bible. Like an ice cream sundae, it is all good. Unlike an ice cream sundae, you can never get too much of the Bible. A newer Christian may want to start in the book of John or the book of 1 John. Psalms and Proverbs declare the wisdom of Heaven. Matthew, Mark, and Luke will build a love for the Lord in a man's heart. The Old Testament is full of stories that will encourage a man to stand for Christ and the New Testament will make a man a blessing to his pastor and his church. It is all good.

Strong Christian lives are not built in a day. The steady Christian who builds a habit of consuming the Word of God will begin to see subtle yet powerful changes in his life. His thinking, his language, his habits, and his desires will slowly be conformed to the heart of God. Temptations that once were certain to knock him down, now are engaged in a battle. When he does fall, he rises more quickly with a fresh determination to win the next encounter. The fire of God's Word smolders in his soul gradually intensifying. Over time, the Bible plants itself in a man's heart, and he becomes fortified in Christ.

On a hot August afternoon in Rustamiyah, Iraq, PFC Brendan Schweigart illustrated the importance of the Bible and a man's heart. A sniper opened fire with his target the soldier's heart, but the bullet missed. Schweigart left the USA with a promise to his mother, saying he would always go into battle with his Bible, and that Bible over his heart was just enough to deflect the bullet from his vital organs. His mother said, "Through the back of the arm, there's a hole going in, a hole coming out, and then one coming into the side of his chest and one coming out."[9] For Schweigart, the Bible was a physical protector; for you and me, the Bible is a spiritual protector against the deadliest of all enemies.

If we will stand against the assaults of Satan, the Bible must dominate our hearts.

Keep your weapon close.

CHAPTER THREE

WHEN THE ENEMY WINS

T he dark shadow of death cast its pall upon the huddled group. The quiet sobbing of a broken-hearted mother was the only sound competing with the mournful music and priestly chants. The baby was dead.

The baby's father might well be a king, but the "wages of sin" (Romans 6:23) is still death. He could even be an individual "after [God's] own heart" (1 Samuel 13:14), an author who could write the "Lord is my shepherd" (Psalm 23:1), a man of faith who could conquer Goliath, but when sin is finished it still "bringeth forth death" (James 1:15). Even the Bible admits there are "the pleasures of sin for a season" (Hebrews 11:25), but that mighty prophet Ezekiel preached it like this: "...the soul that sinneth, it shall die" (Ezekiel 18:4).

There is something unfair about the funeral of this little baby. He had never decided to take a vacation when the kings would "go forth to battle" (2 Samuel 11:1). He had never looked on a woman to lust after her; he had never made a righteous man drunk; he had never ordered the death of a loyal subject in battle; nor had he ever covered his iniquity. The man of God, Nathan, was not pointing at the baby when he said, "…Thou art the man…" (2 Samuel 12:7).

But the little baby bore the consequences of his daddy's sin. When "sin is finished," there are only questions and doubts.

> WHEN "SIN IS FINISHED," THERE ARE ONLY QUESTIONS AND DOUBTS.

Imagine the confidential conversation between David and Bathsheba. "We have sinned against the Lord. We have violated the Bible. We have paid a horrible price." One can almost hear an invited counselor hold their hands and tell them it was time to "move on." The king may well have spoken the words humans are so prone to say, "We will have to put this behind us."

It is wonderful to know from the Bible that there is complete forgiveness from the heart of God. When Nathan said, "…The Lord also hath put away thy sin" (2 Samuel 12:13) there was no compromise in the forgiveness of Heaven. "And their sins and iniquities will I remember no more" (Hebrews 11:17). "…He is faithful and just to forgive us our sins" (1 John 1:9). "…I will pardon all their iniquities..." (Jeremiah 33:8). "...Thou wilt cast all their sins into the depths of the sea" (Micah 7:19).

Forgiveness removes the sin, but there still can be the consequences.

David became the king of Israel at the age of thirty and reigned for forty years. He was probably nearing his fiftieth birthday when he chose to be an adulterer, and the changes to the kingdom are astounding. A casual reading of 1 Samuel 17 through 2 Samuel 10 details one of the most outstanding biographies ever recorded about a human. We read of David's courage and his faith, his compassion and his holiness, his forgiveness and his grace, and his wisdom and his discernment. We see him in times of joyous victory and lonely defeat. We can hear the ladies sing that David has slain "his ten thousands" (1 Samuel 18:7). We watch his own soldiers consider stoning him, yet in every circumstance, righteous David honors his God.

> FORGIVENESS REMOVES THE SIN, BUT THERE STILL CAN BE THE CONSEQUENCES.

Then in one day, everything changed. For twenty years David ruled with the unique blessing of God falling on his kingdom, but when he submitted to the temptation of the evil one, the terrifying transformation would affect every corner of his life. His family slowly crumbled before his very eyes, and there was nothing he could do to stop it. His own children committed disgusting acts of immorality that transcended his own sin with Bathsheba, but David did not have the moral authority to stop them. For twenty years he built a kingdom at which the world would marvel, a kingdom the mightiest armies could never touch, and then he spent twenty excruciating years watching it all fall apart. "We will put this behind us." Easier said than done.

David's psalms give a glimpse into the suffering he experienced after his sin. The titles in the book of Psalms are fascinating. Some of the titles tell us the type of instrument that was used to sing that particular song. Some give background detail as to the events that led to the message in the Psalm. Some were written for certain choirs or individuals to sing. The title of Psalm 38 is powerful. It is "a psalm of David to bring to remembrance."

David is saying, "I have learned some lessons from my sin that I cannot afford to forget. I have reaped consequences that I don't want to reap again. The next time my flesh tells me I am the exception to the rule, I want to be reminded that with every temptation there is a 'way to escape' (1 Corinthians 10:13). I refuse to walk down this path again."

> Sin will take you farther than you want to go,
>
> Cost you more than you want to pay,
>
> And keep you longer than you want to stay.

The roaring lion has an intense ability to make sin look attractive, which he accomplishes in part by hiding the results of wickedness.

When the evil one plunges his fangs into the helpless victim and rips and slashes, the resulting bloody mess looks far different from the promised pleasures of sin. We would do well to "remember."

David's sin had caught up with him. Though the softened ministers of our day would be offended at such a thought, God was dealing with him. David said that God was "rebuking" and "chastening" him. God's rebuke meant that He had already passed judgment of David's sin, and now it was time for the consequences.

Psalm 38:1 expresses David's understanding, and even his fear, that God rebukes and chastens His children. We see the same in Hebrews 12:6, "For whom the Lord loveth he chasteneth, and scourgeth every son whom he receiveth." What potent words the Bible uses, yet what a tender reminder that His powerful correction is predicated on His marvelous care and gracious goodness.

> HIS POWERFUL CORRECTION IS PREDICATED ON HIS MARVELOUS CARE AND GRACIOUS GOODNESS.

He chastens because He loves. He chastens because He wants us to "remember." He cannot let us stray into sin without responding with correction and chastening motivated by His holiness and love.

Verse 1 becomes stronger by the inclusion of the words "hot displeasure." God was greatly displeased with David. Our English phrase "hot displeasure" is one word in the Hebrew Bible, a word that occurs 126 times in the Old Testament. In 103 of those occasions, the word is used in reference to Almighty God. Fury, indignation, wrath, and rage are some of the readings we have describing the God of the Bible.[1] Indeed, the mighty King of Glory does not resemble the weakened deity liberal pastors teach. Read the following paragraphs carefully as we examine God's heart toward sin, and then His heart toward His child.

First, the verses below remind us that God's heart toward sin is fierce. Hear the Word of the Lord! Listen to God's stouthearted servants thunder Bible truth!

The prophet Isaiah cries out, "According to their deeds, accordingly he will repay, fury to his adversaries, recompense to his enemies..." (Isaiah 59:18). Consider the weeping preacher Jeremiah: "And I myself will fight against you with an outstretched hand and with a strong arm, even in anger, and in fury, and in great wrath" (Jeremiah 21:5). God's man Ezekiel is not ashamed to preach, "Therefore will I also deal in fury: mine eye shall not spare, neither will I have pity..." (Ezekiel 8:18). "...I will even rend it with a stormy wind in my fury; and there shall be an overflowing shower in mine anger, and great hailstones in my fury to consume it" (Ezekiel 13:13).

The prophet Micah pronounces, "I will execute vengeance in anger and fury upon the heathen, such as they have not heard" (Micah 5:15). Listen to Nahum: "Who can stand before his indignation? and who can abide in the fierceness of his anger? his fury is poured out like fire, and the rocks are thrown down by him" (Nahum 1:6). Zechariah proclaims, "...I was jealous for her with great fury" (Zechariah 8:2). No wonder he paid for his preaching with his life.

How different are God's preachers in the Bible from the ministers of today. How many people face the consequence of sin because a softened seminarian stands unwilling to sound the alarm. "There is no fear of God before their eyes" (Romans 3:18) because there is no fear of God in the pulpit.

Second, for every believing sinner, God's wrath on sin was completely poured out upon the Lord Jesus Christ on the cross of Calvary! What an astounding consideration—that the God we just read about would dare to pour out the full extent of His wrath and anger upon His Son, in your place! What amazing grace and unspeakable mercy. Truly Calvary was the place where God's truth and justice met God's grace and mercy. "Mercy and truth are met together; righteousness and peace have kissed each other" (Psalm 85:10).

While Calvary may have absorbed God's anger and the full payment of sin, still the painful consequences of sin threaten the life of every child of God—just as they did King David. May those consequences motivate us to flee temptation and resist the devil! Consider the horrible pain and regret that David's choices brought upon his life and the scars his sin created.

As David's sin finds him out, he cries out, "Thine arrows stick fast in me, and thy hand presseth me sore" (Psalm 38:2). Just when David figured all the bases were covered, God pulled back on the bow and shot the arrow of conviction dead center into the target—David's heart. Heaven's arrows are not so easy to pull out, and the lingering effects sunk into David's being. When the Father chastened the son whom He loved, it was not a slap on the wrist, but rather a life-altering experience that no doubt broke the heart of God just as it broke David's heart. It was a chastening time that David would not forget.

The enemy attacked. David buckled. Now he is ready to enumerate what sin had produced in his life. Notice these eighteen statements based on Psalm 38:

> There is no soundness in my flesh.
>
> I can't sleep.
>
> I am in too deep.
>
> The burden is too heavy.
>
> I stink.
>
> I am in trouble.
>
> I am bowed down greatly.
>
> I cannot stop crying.
>
> I am physically sick.
>
> I am feeble and broken.
>
> My heart roars.
>
> I groan all the time.

My heart pants.

My strength is gone.

My friends and family have forsaken me.

My enemies are emboldened.

I am speechless.

My sorrow never leaves me.

David faced consequences for his sin in every area of his life. Physically, his health was so broken that twice he said, "There is no soundness in my flesh." His pus-filled sores brought a stench to the palace halls that must have sickened his servants as they watched their king. Worse must have been the agonizing screams those servants would hear from the king's bedroom. The Bible words are "roaring" and "groaning." Walk the halls of a hospital and one can hear the wail and roar of a man who cannot bear his pain. The next room might well bed a man who cannot sleep, but instead moans and groans through the night. With David, the two are combined; roaring one moment and groaning the next.

DAVID FACED CONSEQUENCES FOR HIS SIN IN EVERY ASPECT OF HIS LIFE.

David's sin gave him a "loathsome disease." It was a sickness in his loins that constantly burned like an out of control fire. His raging fever attacked his mind. The psychological trauma broke him internally as the physical torments broke his body. He couldn't speak; he couldn't hear; he couldn't sleep; and he couldn't shake his sorrow.

Commentator John Philips points out that David's disease caused his wives, his friends, and his family to desert him. David called his disease a "sore" in verse 11, a word most frequently used in the Old Testament with reference to the dreaded disease of leprosy. Mr. Philips concludes that David was for a time a leper, which, had he not been a king, would have forced him to be driven out of the palace, cover his lip, and constantly cry, "Unclean! Unclean!"[2]

What damage the enemy does! Psalm 38 doesn't even remind us of the other consequences David had to endure. His baby died; his daughter was raped by his son; his son was murdered by another son; family members could not speak to each other; his relatives stabbed him in the back; his son led the nation in rebellion against his father; his best friends dealt treacherously against him; his son fornicated on the roof of the palace; many tried to ruin him; and those are only the stories God included in His Word.

The enemy never informs a man on the roof of his house, "If you listen to me I will devastate your life." But after the sin, a disgusted David could only recall the joys of his past days and compare them with the 24-hour misery that now besieged him. He could only tell himself, "The next time temptation is knocking on the door, I am going to remember what it cost me last time. I will never let myself forget the torture of my soul, my flesh, and my family. Until the day I die, I will have burning in my soul the anguish I have brought to my kingdom and to the heart of God."

If there were a smidgen of honesty in him, the crafty one would at least put a warning label on his plots, forcing him to tell of the misery and broken lives he leaves behind. "Warning—this sin will ruin your life. It will destroy your body, it will corrupt your mind, it will excoriate your emotions, and it will bankrupt your future. It will steal your respect and your reason. It will break your will, your marriage, your family, and your life."

When a man has made his choice, it is too late to go back. The best he can do is "remember."

David certainly had the ability to make a colossal mess, but he also had the willingness to clean it up. He learned there are no cheap formulas to "put it behind us," but rather contrite, serious confession is the hope for restoration. Psalm 38 (like Psalm 6, 32, 51, 102, and 130) instructs the child of God in the matter of Bible repentance. Thank God He is "…faithful and just to forgive us our sins, and to cleanse us from all unrighteousness" (1 John 1:9).

WARNING—
THIS SIN WILL
RUIN YOUR LIFE.

Verse 18 contains two critical statements. David said, "I will declare mine iniquity" and "I will be sorry for my sin." When Nathan pointed the finger of conviction at the king, David realized the game was over. He thought he had carefully covered his tracks, but like Achan of old, David forgot to look up when he was hiding his sin. "The eyes of the Lord are in every place, beholding the evil and the good" (Proverbs 15:3). The children's song reminds us adults how the "Father up above is looking down in love, so be careful little hands what you do." That is powerful theology.

When David declared his iniquity, he was simply acknowledging and admitting what God already knew. He was "reporting" the sin, in effect, stating the cover-up was done. The New Testament word *confess* literally means to say along with God that my sin is wrong. We are in agreement with Heaven that our excuses don't work, that our reasons are faulty, and we are responsible for our wrong. David was tired of hiding his sin in his heart, and now it was in the open.

David's being "sorry" was quite different from the common "sorry" of our day. David's "sorry" painted a picture of the fear and anxiety that filled his life from the moment he decided to sin. David's "sorry" went so far as to say, "The next time I am tempted to sin, I am going to think twice." David's "sorry" meant that he was going to walk much more carefully next time.[3]

Every child is "sorry" when his hand is caught in the cookie jar. Everyone is "sorry" that they have been caught. We are "sorry" that our stupidity embarrassed us.

Second Corinthians 7:10–11 gives us the Bible definition of "sorry." "Godly sorrow" is a real sorrow that produces a changed life. "Cookie-jar sorrow" is a temporary sorrow that changes nothing. When a sinner has "godly sorrow," he understands that his "iniquities have separated" (Isaiah 59:2) himself from God. His violations have brought the wrath of God upon him (John 3:36), and the end game is to be "cast into the lake of fire" (Revelation 20:15). Now he cries like the hated tax collector in Luke 18:13, "…God be merciful to me a sinner." He has arrived at the same condition as the thief on the cross who said, "…we receive the due rewards of our deeds" (Luke 23:41).

No wonder that godly sorrow produces a "salvation not to be repented of"! When a man has this type of repentance, he will follow the Lord in believer's baptism. He will become faithful to a local church. He will have a heart to give. He will have a hatred for sin. You might even say he has become a "new creature" (2 Corinthians 5:17).

Surface sorrow or regret alone does not save. Many have called out to God for "help" but that falls far short of biblical salvation. For instance, consider a man whose life is dominated by sin. He is a drunk, a thief, a fornicator, and a gambler. He is full of envy, pride, raging anger, and filthy thoughts. He sees his sin is costing his marriage, and when his wife is ready to leave him, he crawls into the pastor's office feeling "sorry." He wants Jesus to "help" him so he can keep his wife. If that means he has to pray a "sinner's prayer" so be it. He will do whatever is necessary to keep his marriage. Rather than seeing his need for a Saviour, he's merely asking God for a temporary fix—a relief valve from the consequences of his sin.

Bible salvation and a true heart of repentance do not say, "God assist me." Bible salvation says, "God, save me!"

A Christian exhibiting a godly sorrow for sin has an intense desire to be "clear." Second Corinthians 7:11 gives the results of godly sorrow. Here is the list:

- It brings "carefulness" (an earnestness to get right with God now rather than later).
- It brings a "clearing of yourselves" (a desire to make a defense; my sins are gone).
- It brings an "indignation" (an anger for what sin has produced).
- It brings a "fear" (a terror of what is left when sin runs its course).
- It brings a "vehement desire" (an intense reaction to sin).
- It brings a "zeal" (a hot fervency to do right).
- It brings a "revenge" (a desire for justice).[4]

No wonder God wanted David to place Psalm 38 in the songbook of the Bible. No wonder He wanted saints of all ages to be warned about the consequences of sin. No wonder He wanted His children to have a Bible example of confession.

No wonder He wants us to "remember."

As a young Italian artist, Leonardo da Vinci painted a beautiful portrait of a young child appearing as an angel. The artist was so pleased with his work that he kept it in his studio where he might gaze upon it. When he was troubled, a look at the painting brought comfort to his soul and calmed his anger.

Years later, da Vinci wanted to paint an opposite picture of a man personifying evil. A long and diligent search produced a model with facial features that had been scarred and ruined by sin. Truly, the model was the polar opposite of the young, angelic child.

When the bitter, angry man entered the studio he told the artist that he was also the model for the beautiful canvas painted years earlier. Decades of crime and sin had taken a countenance of peace and solemnity and replaced it with hatred and vindictiveness. The two canvasses told an amazing story of a ruined life.[5]

When the enemy wins, the scars that remain on our lives, our marriages, our homes, and our churches are horrific. The innocent past is replaced by a tormented present leading to a tragic future. Satan is on the prowl. He is lurking in the tall grass. He is looking for another victim to devour. He wants to paint the last picture of our lives.

David has some advice: "Remember."

CHAPTER FOUR

THE ENEMY AND HIS DEVICES

W hat is it about the cheese and the mousetrap? We have all heard the story of the sweet mother mouse warning her little rodent of the dangers of the trap. The diminutive know-it-all soon decides that his life experiences are greater than good ole mom and cautiously converges on the enticing chunk of cheese. A sniff becomes a lick which turns into a nibble and then a good, healthy bite, and one more little mouse bites the dust. If a little mouse will ever become a big mouse, he needs to stay away from the trigger on the trap.

The cheese and the trigger have a counterpart in the Bible. In the Greek New Testament, the word sounds like this: *skándalon*. One Greek scholar gives the word this definition: "The trigger of a trap on which the bait is placed, and which, when touched by the animal, springs and causes it to close, causing entrapment. Skándalon involves a reference also to the conduct of the person who is thus trapped. Skándalon always denotes an enticement to conduct which could ruin the person in question."[1]

When the word is translated in our King James Bible, it usually reads as the word *offence* (offense), *offend*, or *stumbling block*. Like the mother mouse, the Bible faithfully instructs us to be on guard for the enticement the enemy brings into our lives to entrap us. The offense is not just the trigger on the trap that slams its victim senseless; it is also our actions that lead to our destruction. When we decide to smell the bait, lick the bait, nibble on the bait, and bite the bait, we are contributing to the offense. The roaring lion says, "Give it a try—you can always back off later." The Saviour says, "Abstain from all appearance of evil" (1 Thessalonians 5:22).

This is yet one more insidious truth about the enemy. He is a roaring lion on the path of destruction, but he is also a crafty serpent baiting a trap. Patiently, carefully he looks for snares and entrapments that will lure a man to the place where the trap springs shut. No wonder the Bible warns us not to be "ignorant of his devices" (2 Corinthians 2:11). His "devices" are carefully thought out schemes luring a man to the pitfalls of his own destruction.

The Bible identifies a number of such offenses the enemy uses to ensnare his victims. For the unsaved man, these are traps he uses to control a man ultimately bringing eternal damnation in Hell.

For the Christian, these are traps designed to destroy a testimony, a family, a marriage, or a church. It is such serious business with the Saviour that He said, "Woe unto the world because of offenses! for it must needs be that offenses come; but woe to that man by whom the offense cometh!" (Matthew 18:7)

THE ENEMY USES THE OFFENSE OF WORLDLY THINKING

Peter was quite the character. He epitomizes so many of us with his uncanny ability of opening his mouth and inserting his foot at just the wrong time. From his silly idea of building tabernacles at the transfiguration of Christ, to the disgraceful, profanity-laced denial of the Son of God, the story of Peter is the story of a man impressed with his own credentials. When reading the New Testament, one cannot help but hear Peter inserting himself into every situation, and when Jesus is looking for a response, it more often than not was Peter's opinions that were forthcoming.

In the Gospels, Peter's finest hour would have to be Matthew 16:16. It seems the pollsters must have had a field day with Jesus as He traversed the land, for He asked His disciples, "…Whom do men say that I the Son of man am?" (Matthew 18:13). Can you hear the disciples answer, "Well, Lord, there was an article about that in last week's edition of Israel Today. It seems that 31% of the respondents say you are John the Baptist, 27% claim you are

Elijah, another 22% said you are Jeremiah, 15% said you are another prophet, and 5% were unsure." (5% are always unsure.)

"Lord, we have been tracking the daily Rasmussen Poll. There is bad news, and there is good news. The bad news is that your approval rating is on a steady decline, but the good news is that the Pharisees' approval numbers are falling even more rapidly."

Jesus then asks the question of the ages. "...But whom say ye that I am?" (Matthew 16:15). The single greatest choice a man will make in his life stems from his opinion of Christ. Who is He to you? If He is only a prophet, a gracious man, a revolutionary, a leader of men, He cannot be your Saviour. Your answer to this question will determine your eternity in Heaven or Hell. "Whom say ye that I am?"

> THE SINGLE GREATEST CHOICE A MAN WILL MAKE IN HIS LIFE STEMS FROM HIS OPINION OF CHRIST.

We should not be surprised when Peter steps to the plate to answer the question of the ages. It was not the respected man of social stature John, nor the fiery zealot Simon, nor the guileless Nathanael, nor the thoughtful Jude, but impetuous Simon Peter, the son of Jonah. And in ten words, the man hits a grand slam. Human words could not say it more succinctly or correctly. "...Thou art the Christ, the Son of the Living God" (Matthew 16:16). Absolutely perfect!

The Saviour responds, "Blessed art thou" (Matthew 16:17). In less than twenty seconds, Jesus would tell Peter that He (Christ) would build His church so that all the forces of Hell could not stop it, and that he (Peter and ultimately the other disciples) would be given the "keys of the kingdom of heaven" (Matthew 16:19), to open Heaven's door to sinners around the world. What a moment in the life of the Galilean fisherman! Imagine hearing such words.

It took Peter a full four verses to make a mess of things. Jesus began to prophesy of His suffering and death alarming Peter to the point that he literally grabbed the Saviour's hand and pulled Him aside. He went on to "rebuke" the "Christ, the Son of the living God" telling him in no uncertain terms, "…this shall not be unto thee" (Matthew 16:22).

Listen to our Lord's response: "…Get thee behind me Satan, for thou art an offence unto me…" (Matthew 16:23). So much for "Blessed art thou."

Despite his honorable and sincere intentions, Peter was being used of Satan to be an offense to Christ. The wicked one was trying to cause the Saviour to stumble on Calvary's road, and he was using the human logic and reasoning of one of His closest associates. Jesus used one powerful word in Matthew 16:23 to expose Satan's tactics and Peter's weakness. He said, "thou savourest not the things that be of God, but those that be of men." *Savourest* refers to the mindset and thinking that was dominating Peter. His problem stemmed from the truth that he did not savor the "things that be of God," but rather, he was following the thinking "of men."

Human reasoning would validate Peter's rebuke. Certainly, the logician would understand Peter's thought process in stating that death cannot be in the vocabulary of the one who is Life. The soldier would readily join Peter's call to arms to defend the King of kings. The common man who heard Him "gladly" (Mark 12:37) would reject such a message that would upset his meal ticket. The deaf who heard, the blind who saw, the lepers cleansed, the dead raised to life again, and the possessed set free could never comprehend such an ugly and horrific end for the one who embodied grace, love, and mercy.

But that is the problem. Peter's thinking was human thinking and God's thinking is vastly different. "For my thoughts are not your thoughts, neither are your ways my ways, saith the LORD" (Isaiah 55:8). Frequently, human thinking contradicts heavenly thinking, and a man who chooses his thinking over God's thinking instantly becomes an offense.

Listen to the Apostle Paul preaching in Corinth, the Las Vegas of his day. With the scholarly Greek professors as well as the intently religious Jews tuning in, he boldly tells them, "It is 'Christ crucified' (1 Corinthians 1:23). He is your only hope for salvation. It is His precious blood that washes sins away. He is 'the way, the truth and the life' (John 14:6)." There were no fancy words and slick packages to make his message palatable. In fact, his preaching lacked excellent speech and wisdom. He was weak and trembling when he preached, to the point that his words were "contemptible" (2 Corinthians 10:10). But, oh, were they powerful!

How easily we can hear the university professors shake their heads in disbelief. "You mean to say that I need the blood given on a cross to wash my sins away? Sir, this 'slaughter house religion' of yours is too simplistic, too gory, and too distasteful for a dignified lot like us." Certainly, the response of religion would be similar. "We have our beautiful halls of worship replete with reverential music and ravishing artwork. We have spent our lives following laws and instructions

A MAN WHO CHOOSES HIS THINKING OVER GOD'S THINKING INSTANTLY BECOMES AN OFFENSE.

to impress God with our goodness. Now you are telling us that we are sinners in need of repentance and forgiveness. You are claiming my religious relics and good works cannot please God, and that it is not by our works of righteousness. I am offended by your insolent attitude. God will accept me just the way I am!"

First Corinthians 1:23 says it like this: "But we preach Christ crucified, unto the Jews a stumbling block, and unto the Greeks foolishness." Hell is loaded with sinners who stumbled their way in because they allowed human thinking to supersede Bible thinking. A young person sitting in a university hall listening to a teacher mock God and exalt his own humanistic ideas would do well to cry out, "Thou art an offense unto me!" The religious man trusting systems and schemes, who has accepted dictates of popes and prophets instead of the Bible would do well to inform his parson, "Thou art an offense unto me!" The seminary student soaking in the boastful rants of a Hell-bound teacher who corrects the Bible should be crying out, "Thou art an offense unto me!"

Human thinking has not only damned souls to Hell, it has also ruined untold numbers of saints. Abraham made a series of damaging choices when "Because I thought" (Genesis 20:11) became more important than God's promises. Moses thought he could pick and choose which commands to implicitly follow, and he assumed God would never keep him out of the Promised Land. Uzza thought his sincere desire to protect the ark of God would override the Bible command to never touch holy things. Uzziah thought he was big enough, successful enough, and strong enough to enter in the temple and offer sacrifices. Every time human presumption exalted itself above the Word of God, disaster was right around the corner.

The world tells us, "You are what you eat." But God says it differently. He says, "You are what you think."

> *"For as he thinketh in his heart, so is he...."*
> —PROVERBS 23:7

> *"The thoughts of the righteous are right...."*
> —PROVERBS 12:5

"Commit thy works unto the Lord, and thy thoughts shall be established."—PROVERBS 16:3

"...whatsoever things are true, whatsoever things are honest, whatsoever things are just, whatsoever things are pure, whatsoever things are lovely, whatsoever things are of good report...think on these things."
—PHILIPPIANS 4:8

Psychologists claim that 10,000 thoughts run through the human mind on a daily basis, or more than 3.5 million thoughts per year![2] The battle of the mind is a struggle that never rests, a battle the enemy constantly employs. Lustful thoughts, angry thoughts, depressing thoughts, vengeful thoughts, jealous thoughts, and hateful thoughts are a few of the bullets biding time in his gun.

The Apostle Paul recognized these unseen struggles in the lives of the Corinthian church members and set out to equip them. In 2 Corinthians 10:3-4, he reminds them of the spiritual nature of the conflict.

EVERY TIME HUMAN PRESUMPTION EXALTED ITSELF ABOVE THE WORD OF GOD, DISASTER WAS RIGHT AROUND THE CORNER.

The walk is in the "flesh" but the war is not. This is not a brief, momentary incident, but warfare that lasts a lifetime. "General Paul" lays the maps and the charts on the table and presents the battle plan to bring down the destructive "strongholds" (fortresses).

The Corinthians understood that word picture. Overlooking the city was a hill nearly 1,900 feet high famous for its fortress.[3] The view from the city presented an impregnable force no enemy could conquer. Often, the hidden turmoil of the mind overwhelms the child of God until all hope is gone. "My struggle is as big as that fort on top of that mountain!" But the Bible tells us how the massive citadel on the towering mountain can be pulled down.

> *"Casting down imaginations, and every high thing that exalteth itself against the knowledge of God, and bringing into captivity every thought to the obedience of Christ."*—2 Corinthians 10:5

Notice the two verbs:

There must be a **"casting down."** In other Scriptures the word is used to describe the demolishing of a building or the destruction of an army. When my ideas contradict the ideas of God, my ideas must be obliterated. When my philosophy opposes God's way I must eradicate my plans. When I am convinced that my "high thing" (my proud conclusion) is worthy to be exalted over the knowledge of God, I must then wipe it out. Victory comes when I understand there is no compromise, there is no "meeting of the minds," and His ways are always higher than human ways (Isaiah 55:8).

There must be a **"bringing into captivity."** Now it is time to take some prisoners. Thoughts of pride, anger, envy, revenge, depression and the like must be put behind bars and locked up. We do that by bowing our knee to Christ and surrendering our lives in obedience to Him. The simple word we teach our children is not so simple a strategy, but it is critical. There still is "no other way" but to "trust and obey."

VICTORY COMES WHEN I UNDERSTAND THERE IS NO COMPROMISE, AND HIS WAYS ARE ALWAYS HIGHER THAN HUMAN WAYS.

One little nibble and one little bite is all it takes to spring the trap. When our thinking becomes bigger than God's Word, the next sound we are going to hear is a trap slamming shut.

THE ENEMY USES THE OFFENSE OF DIVISIVE CHURCH MEMBERS

There is a great danger lurking in every local church. We have heard disgraceful stories of churches destroyed by immorality, adultery, fornication, and fleshly sins. We have heard the disgusting tales of ministers who are nothing more than modern day Balaams with a "for sale" sign hung around their necks. We see the churches that once boldly stood for God's Word and salvation by grace alone that now have new "whippersnapper" preachers who believe none of the above. But there is another danger simmering under the radar of even the finest churches. It is so destructive that God spends an alarming portion of the New Testament warning pastors and churches. We find it in Romans 16:17–18:

> "Now I beseech you, brethren, mark them which cause divisions and offenses contrary to the doctrine which ye have learned; and avoid them. For they that are such serve not our Lord Jesus Christ, but their own belly; and by good words and fair speeches deceive the hearts of the simple."

Watch out for the loud-mouthed church members.

They do not promote the "lust of concupiscence" (1 Thessalonians 4:5). They do not stand in pulpits "denying the only Lord God, and our Lord Jesus Christ" (Jude 4). They do not make "merchandise" (2 Peter 2:3) of God's people. But they are incredibly destructive.

The letter to the local church of Rome is not the only one to include such a warning. In Acts 6 there was an ongoing battle between the Grecians and the Hebrews about which widows got the bigger fruit basket on Thanksgiving. First Corinthians 1:10 pleads that "there be no divisions among you." Second Corinthians has dozens of verses in which Paul deals with the rumor mill that gossiped about his work and motives. The story of Galatians is the story of division that came from the dissembling Jews joining

Peter in refusing to eat with Gentiles. The Ephesians were told to "keep the unity of the Spirit in the bond of peace" (Ephesians 4:3). The Philippians had the dynamic duo of Euodias and Syntyche. Colossians 3:13 tells us there were quarrels in that church. The church at Thessalonica heard it twice. "...be at peace among yourselves" (1 Thessalonians 5:13), and "...we hear there are some that walk among you disorderly...busybodies" (2 Thessalonians 3:11).

There are 242 verses in 1 and 2 Timothy and Titus comprising the blueprint for behavior in the local church. Incredibly, divisive people in the assembly are dealt with in forty-nine of the verses, making division the most common theme in these pastoral letters. One fifth of the verses deal with vain jangling, fables, tattlers, busybodies, perverse disputers, babblings, liars, evil beasts, slow bellies, foolish questions, contentions, strivings about the law, and similar subjects. Dividers like Hymenaeus, Alexander, Philetus, Demas, and Alexander the coppersmith, are named and exposed, and it is done without soft language or apology. It would be correct to conclude the Apostle Paul saw the offenses in the local church as a far greater risk and danger than the government in Rome.

THE APOSTLE PAUL SAW THE OFFENSES IN THE LOCAL CHURCH AS A FAR GREATER RISK AND DANGER THAN THE GOVERNMENT IN ROME.

In Philemon, the burning issue stemmed over a wealthy man's willingness to forgive a slave. The Hebrew Christians were reminded to "Obey them that have the rule over you and submit yourselves…" (Hebrews 13:7). The book of James hammers the attitude seen in legions of churches where "respect of persons" (James 2:1) created distinctions and classes between the rich and poor. These attitudes have absolutely no place in God's local church. James also deals with the little issue of "wars and fightings among you" (James 4:1), and he warns them to "Speak not evil one of another…" (James 4:11). That local church must have had some great business meetings!

First Peter tells the saints to be "…of one mind, having compassion one of another, love as brethren, be pitiful, be courteous" (1 Peter 3:8). Second Peter says there shall be "false teachers among you" (2 Peter 2:1). First John is loaded with admonitions regarding local church dividers, proclaiming "Whosoever hateth his brother is a murderer…" (1 John 2:15), and "If a man say, I love God, and hateth his brother, he is a liar…" (1 John 4:20). Nice soft preaching, eh?

Second John warns about "deceivers" (2 John 7), Jude warns of "murmurers, complainers, walking after their own lusts" (Jude 16), and even in the book of Revelation, the local church of Thyatira was warned of a Jezebel in its midst teaching members to "commit fornication, and to eat things sacrificed unto idols" (Revelation 2:20).

Then there is the potent case of 3 John. Certainly it would take a lot to rile the Apostle John—the devoted, affectionate pastor.

Listen as he writes to the "…well-beloved Gaius, whom I love in the truth" (3 John 1). John so loved his people that he said the greatest joy in his life was watching his "children walk in truth" (3 John 4).

It would take a tidal wave of selfishness to enrage this gracious man of God, yet Diotrephes found a way. He so infuriated John, the forgiving pastor stated, "…I will remember his deeds which he doeth…" (3 John 10). He exposed the actions of this hypocrite, a man who prated with "malicious words." The word "prate" refers to a babbler, someone engaged in idle talk. Diotrephes did not call a massive church business meeting to call out the sins of the pastor, but instead, he engaged in water cooler talk. These seemingly idle and innocent words had a purpose, for this ungodly hypocrite refused to "receive the brethren" going so far as to cast them "out of the church."

It would be safe to assume that Diotrephes hid his sin under the cover of some great concern for doctrine or a willingness to stand for right. But John exposes the truth. For all of the self righteous claims, the bottom line was this: he "loveth to have the preeminence among them" (3 John 9). When all the phony talk is stripped away, that is always the single thing left. Offenders love the preeminence. They have to be number one. It is not for "me to live is Christ" (Philippians 1:21), but rather, for "me to live is me." They have no concern about the members that are ruined or the unsaved that are rejected.

From Acts through Revelation, every one of the twenty-three books in the Bible deals with some form of division in the local church. Some dividers were teachers, some were gossipers, some promoted fleshly sins, some fostered hidden spiritual sins, but they are the offenders. They are miserable wretches living in a constant state of despair. They criticize every genuine effort for Christ, they censure those who work for Christ, and they condemn every gain for Christ. They are fault-finding, Pharisaical, phonies who discourage new converts, doubt every program, and damage a church's reputation.

They are in every church and they are in your church. When a person grabs a cup of coffee with one of these offenders, take time to sniff the air. There will be a definite odor of cheese. Converse with them, chuckle with them, consort with them, and soon the back-stabbing knife comes out.

The next sound heard is the sound of a little baby mouse taking it in the neck.

THE ENEMY USES THE OFFENSE OF MORAL SINS

If the average church attendee were to actually read the entire Sermon on the Mount, he would be stunned. The message that begins with gracious words of encouragement inspiring the child of God to experience the favor of God, suddenly becomes a thundering rebuke of counterfeit religion. The very message that contains the model prayer of our Saviour, the "golden rule," and the story of the "wise man who built his house on the rock," is loaded with preaching on Hell, condemnation of hypocrites, and exposition of false ministers and prophets.

A reading of the 107 verses composing the Sermon on the Mount would reveal these timeless instructions: "Ye are the salt of the earth;" "Let your light so shine before men;" "turn to him the other [cheek];" "Love your enemies;" "lay up for yourselves treasures in Heaven;" "seek ye first the Kingdom of God;" "Judge not, that ye be not judged;" "Ask, and it shall be given you" (Matthew 5:13; 5:16; 5:39; 5:44; 6:20; 6:33; 7:1; 7:7).

But the same perusal would also leave the reader with these pronouncements: "ye shall in no case enter into the kingdom of Heaven;" "danger of hell fire;" "as the hypocrites do;" "Be not ye therefore like unto them;" "how great is that darkness;" "Give not that which is holy unto the dogs;" "I never knew you: depart from me, ye that work iniquity" (Matthew 5:20; 5:22; 6:2; 6:8; 6:23; 7:6; 7:23).

Unquestionably, the average church member has heard the former statements quoted far more often than the latter. Yet in the same message in which Jesus comforts His children by elaborating that God will "clothe you" (Matthew 6:30), He also hammers against divorce. With the wonderful reminder "take…no thought for the morrow" (Matthew 6:34) ringing in the ears of the disciples,

He rebukes the critic who sees the mote (a splinter) in the other guy's eye but can't see the beam running out of his own eye. After He reminds His own that the Heavenly Father gives "good things to them that ask him" (Matthew 7:11), the Saviour preaches about a "strait" gate and a "narrow" way (Matthew 7:14).

If the average pastor in America were to preach like Jesus did on the Sermon on the Mount on a Sunday morning at 11:30, he would be a former pastor by noon.

> WHAT YOU ARE IS INFINITELY MORE IMPORTANT THAN WHAT YOU DO.

When Jesus finished this sermon, the "astonished" people knew they had just heard from "one having authority" (Matthew 7:28–29). He never backed down, He never compromised the message, He never feared the religious authoritarians, and He never softened His language. There was a reason, and it is the same reason that separates the modern day 'minister' from the mighty man of God. It is the distinction between the man who knows what his professor says and the man who knows what the Bible says.

Jesus believed in Hell.

He did not believe in a Hell that was simply the grave. He did not accept a Hell that was a place where men were thirsting after God. He did not believe that Hell was a place of annihilation. He believed in a real Hell.

If the book of Matthew were the only place where the Bible dealt with the subject of Hell, it would be enough to terrify any rational person. The word *Hell* is found nine times in our Bible in the book of Matthew, and during each occasion, it issues from the tongue of the Son of God. One of these statements alone ought to rattle the very souls of saints and sinners, but when read concurrently, it is terrorizing. Here is what Jesus believed about Hell:

> "...*whosoever shall say, Thou fool, shall be in danger of hell fire.*"—MATTHEW 5:22

> "...*not that thy whole body should be cast into hell.*" —MATTHEW 5:29

> "...*not that thy whole body should be cast into hell.*" —MATTHEW 5:30

> "...*fear him which is able to destroy both soul and body in hell.*"—MATTHEW 10:28

> "...*thou Capernaum...shalt be brought down to hell...*"—MATTHEW 11:23

> "...*the gates of hell shall not prevail against it.*" —MATTHEW 16:18

> "...*rather than having two eyes to be cast into hell fire.*"—MATTHEW 18:9

"...ye make him twofold more the child of hell than yourselves."—MATTHEW 23:15

"Ye serpents, ye generation of vipers, how can ye escape the damnation of hell?"—MATTHEW 23:33

And for good measure:

"And shall cast them into a furnace of fire: there shall be wailing and gnashing of teeth." —MATTHEW 13:42

"...Depart from me, ye cursed, into everlasting fire, prepared for the devil and his angels:" —MATTHEW 25:41

There stands the reason Jesus wept. There stands the reason "he was moved with compassion" (Matthew 9:36). There stands the reason He went to a "place called Golgotha" (Matthew 27:33). He believed in Hell. And more than anything else, He wanted to be sure humans would not go to Hell.

In Matthew 5:27, Jesus continues the mighty theme of the Sermon on the Mount—Who you are is more important than what you do. He reminds His listeners that the Ten Commandments explicitly said, "Thou shalt not commit adultery." Then He takes it a step further. He explains that a man may not commit adultery with his physical body, but if he looks on a woman with a lustful heart, he has already "committed adultery...in his heart." Sins of the mind prelude the sins of the flesh. Who you are is infinitely more important than what you do.

Now the Saviour delivers an intense warning. "And if thy right eye offend thee, pluck it out." "If thy right hand offend thee, cut it off." Hell is so dreadful, a person would be better losing their body members and go to Heaven than keep those members and wind up in Hell. And to think that some ministers claim there is no fire in Hell!

Once again the searchlight of the Scriptures shines on the enemy's plan. He has long been in the business of using any fleshly, moral sin to drag a person to Hell. Multitudes have gone to the eternal furnace of fire because they were so infatuated with lust and pornography they refused Calvary's forgiveness, choosing sin over the Saviour. They would prefer to keep their sordid affairs, their dirty movies and magazines, and their wicked websites than have Jesus save them.

> YOUR SOUL IS MORE IMPORTANT THAN YOUR PLEASURE.

It is their great "offense." It is the one thing more important in their lives than forgiveness. It is the one thing that they are convinced is worth going to Hell for. When a man trusts Christ as his Saviour, he is trusting Jesus to wash his sins away. No one will ever get to Heaven by quitting his sins, yet when someone is saved, he is asking Him to wash his sins away. A man who wants his sin more than a Saviour is a man who is not ready to be saved. Therein lies the great choice a sinner has to make, "Do I want my sin or do I want a Saviour to wash my sins away." A man who chooses that one sin over the Saviour has identified the "offense."

Remember that Christ is preaching this sermon to His disciples (Matthew 5:1). He wants them to watch out for the fraudulent professionalism that was so prevalent in the lives of the religious hierarchy of the day. They were to examine their own lives to be certain of their own standing with God. Unless their righteousness exceeded the righteousness of the scribes and Pharisees, "ye shall in no case enter into the kingdom of heaven" (Matthew 5:20). Twenty-five years later, the Apostle Paul would write to a church full of presumed Christians with a similar warning. "Examine yourselves, whether ye be in the faith; prove your own selves" (2 Corinthians 13:5).

> WHEN SATAN CAN RUIN A MAN MORALLY HE DESTROYS MUCH MORE THAN AN INDIVIDUAL LIFE.

The Sermon on the Mount becomes a great place for man to take spiritual stock of his life. Am I playing religion or am I trusting in Christ alone (Matthew 7:15)? Is my confidence in my own failed attempts at righteousness or am I clinging to the righteousness of Christ (Matthew 5:20)? Does the fruit of my life prove my standing with Christ or does my life preach a different message (Matthew 7:16–19)? Do I truly know Him, and more importantly, does He know me (Matthew 7:23)?

How frightening that a man can walk with Christ, listen to Christ preach, work miracles in the name of Christ, and even preach about Christ, yet not know Him. Of Judas Iscariot, the hypocrite of the ages, Jesus said these words: "good were it for that man if he had never been born" (Mark 14:21). Whether a man is a church member or the town drunk, the message from Christ is crystal clear. Don't let a sin drag you into Hell. Your soul is more important than your pleasure.

There is a message for the other eleven disciples here. The Sermon on the Mount is, by biblical standards, a very lengthy message because Jesus wants His disciples to recognize the danger of moral sin in their lives. While it is true these offenses can blind a lost man to the Gospel, they can also turn a soulwinning, Bible-reading, church-attending, tithing man into a Pharisee.

There were many good traits to be admired in Pharisees. They knew the Bible and could quote hundreds of verses. They wore very modest clothes that testified of their piety. They were committed to their families and they were generous givers. They had a heritage dating to the prophet Ezra that was to be admired. But they were also the arch-enemies of the Son of God.

The Pharisees had crossed a line. Instead of concentrating on the God who "knoweth the secrets of the heart" (Psalm 44:21), they became engrossed in impressing people. By their dress, their praying, their giving, and their fasting, they were able to convince their fellow citizens of their passionate devotion to God. One lie built on another and soon the game of the hypocrite became a full-time job. On the outside they were attractive and impressive, but on the inside they were "full of dead men's bones" (Matthew 23:27).

Jesus is pleading with the disciples to understand that all of the outward dress and moral standards and holy words mean nothing if the inside is filthy. When Satan can ruin a man morally he destroys much more than an individual life. He gets a marriage, a family, and oftentimes a ministry. He gives occasion for the enemies to laugh at and mock the man who preached one thing and lived another. No wonder he saves his best offenses for the moral battles that wage deep in a man's mind and heart.

In the middle of the Sermon on the Mount, Jesus alerts the disciples to the moral triggers that will spring the trap and shatter a life. As the alarm is sounding, the Saviour gives the righteous man some insight in doing battle with a great hot spot in the spiritual war. Here is His advice:

Watch your heart. Jesus told His disciples that a man who "looketh on a woman to lust after her" had already committed adultery where it really mattered—"in his heart" (Matthew 5:28). The "look of lust" is an intensive, passionate gaze that causes a man to want what is not his. Whether or not the "look" turns into a physical sin does not change the fact that the violation has occurred in the heart. Victory comes when a righteous man surrenders his eyes to the Lord and begs for the character and discipline to say with Job, "I made a covenant with mine eyes; why then should I think upon a maid?" (Job 31:1).

Watch your eyes. If a man's eyes cause him to stumble, it would be better to "pluck" them out and "cast" them away (Matthew 5:29). In our society, waging war with the "lust of the eyes" (1 John 2:16) is a constant tussle. It is impossible to escape the billboards and posters and immodest dress that permeate our land. Victory comes when a righteous man follows the command of Proverbs 4:25: "Let thine eyes look right on, and let thine eyelids look straight before thee."

Watch your hands. In Matthew 5:30, Jesus states that a man would be better cutting his hand off than allowing it to ruin his life. When a man sins with his hands it is always intentional. Hands that grab a remote control and tune to a wicked movie channel have made a conscious choice. Fingers that type the address of a salacious website are following the wishes of a dirty mind. Victory is only possible when we

OTHERS BEFORE HAVE WON THE VICTORY AND YOU CAN TOO.

understand our sinful flesh and determine to fight. "But every man is tempted, when he is drawn away of his own lust, and enticed" (James 1:14).

The conflict of the righteous man is a ferocious engagement of powerful forces. There is no prescription or pill that can transform a frail Christian into a soldier ready to fight. The simple answer is the only answer—a man must have the character to say "no" to sin.

Colossians 3:5 tells the man of God to "mortify" filthy appetites and wicked obsessions. Fight it! Beat it! Kill it!

> *"There hath no temptation taken you but such as is common to man: but God is faithful, who will not suffer you to be tempted above that ye are able; but will with the temptation also make a way to escape, that ye may be able to bear it."*
> —1 CORINTHIANS 10:13

You can say "no." You can walk away. You can look away. You can turn off the TV. You can shut down the computer. You can find the way to escape. You can bear it. Others before have won the victory and you can too.

Years ago I sat as a young preacher at a lunch table with a 'seasoned' saint. He told me that decades earlier, he had planted a church in a western state and seen the power of God in a remarkable way. Many were saved, families were transformed, marriages repaired, and a church rapidly grew. For a young pastor, life was good, and he relished the favor of God.

One day, unexpectedly, unannounced, moral sin was knocking at the door. The conviction of the Bible told him to say "no" and the lust of the flesh told him to say "yes." Many would laugh at the simplicity of such a statement, yet, for all the analysis, sermons, and moralizing, it always comes down to a moment of time—the moment a man says "yes" or "no." The young pastor said, "Yes."

Fifty years later I sat at a table listening to his story. Huge, round tears flowed down his face as he described the shame, the disgrace, and the pain. Saying "yes" cost him his ministry, his wife, his family, and his reputation. Repeatedly, he would weep and softly say, "It wasn't worth it. It wasn't worth it."

Sin is a choice. Victory is a choice. Make your choice.

There is an enemy walking about seeking "whom he may devour." He has a boatload of offenses that he uses to entice people into his trap. When a man begins to play with sin, pamper himself with sin, entice himself with sin, he is playing right into the wicked one's playbook.

"Smell the cheese. Taste the cheese. Bite the cheese." The closer a man gets to the trigger on the trap, the deeper the danger becomes. And just when he thinks himself to be strong enough to handle the situation, the next sound heard is the sound of a hard lesson being learned. Satan is not playing games.

The story is told of a king hiring a man to drive his carriage. Three applicants were chosen to receive an interview. The first individual was asked by the king, "If you are my driver, how close can you come to the edge of the cliff without falling over?" The man responded, "I can come within twelve inches of the edge of the cliff and still control the carriage."

The second individual told the king, "I am able to drive the carriage within six inches of the edge of the cliff and not fall over."

Impressed with the driving abilities of the first two candidates, the king asked the third man how close he could drive the coach to the edge of the cliff. He responded, "Sire, we will never know. If I am driving the coach carrying his royal highness, I shall stay as far as humanly possible from the edge of the cliff."

Guess who got the gig?

Stay away from the cheese.

CHAPTER FIVE

GOING TO BATTLE
AGAINST THE ENEMY

Something special sits in the soul of a soldier who wants to be in the hottest part of the battle. The analysts, critics, and commentators opine incessantly in endless numbers, but rare is the man who lets his actions speak instead of his words. Every army needs its hero.

The Lord's army has such a soldier, an angel by the name of Michael. Three Bible incidents detail the courage of this prodigious warrior who constantly defends his King and Kingdom. Not only has Michael built an impressive résumé of victories, his greatest is yet to come. There is good reason the General of generals has placed the title "archangel" upon him. He has earned his medals. He has earned his rank.

Michael's first encounter took place over the body of Moses. "Yet Michael the archangel, when contending with the devil he disputed about the body of Moses, durst not bring against him a railing accusation, but said, The Lord rebuke thee" (Jude 9). The long life of humble Moses had come to an end, and God buried him in a valley in the land of Moab. Realizing the penchant for humans to create shrines that deify great men, Moses was buried so that "no man (knew) of his sepulchre" (Deuteronomy 34:6). But a fascinating battle develops. For reasons unknown to humans, God evidently had further intentions for the body of Moses. When Satan decided to hinder those plans, Michael contended with the wicked one.

Michael's second skirmish centers over the "greatly beloved" Daniel (Daniel 9:23). An intensely powerful vision has broken the prophet to the point of mourning, and for three weeks he cannot eat. At last, the mighty messenger from glory has arrived with the astonishing end-time prophecies. Flesh and blood did not witness this battle, but this encounter of "spiritual wickedness in high places" (Ephesians 6:12) must have been an event for the ages. Lasting twenty-one days, Satan and his cohorts resisted the words of God intended for Daniel, but the faithful prayers of God's man provided the weaponry, and Michael supplied the forces. The victory was won.

The words of most humans seem to be caught up in the din and hubbub of mortal activity. They have little or no impact and rarely create an impression worth remembering. But on occasion, a man rises with the ability to clearly articulate and motivate. As with E.F. Hutton, when such a man speaks, people listen. The voice of God's archangel must be such a voice, for the return of Jesus in the clouds will feature the "voice of the archangel" (1 Thessalonians 4:16). The shout from glory will get the attention of his saints. General Michael will give the command to "Come up hither" (Revelation 4:1); the trump of God will resound; and when we all see Jesus, we will sing and shout the victory. The trusted, proven, faithful Michael will stand guard as thousands of thousands are caught up in the clouds "to meet the Lord in the air" (1 Thessalonians 4:17). What a scene that will be!

Michael's past battles empower him for his greatest conflict yet to come. It is found in Revelation 12, where Pastor John witnesses not a world war but a heavenly war. As the tribulation period unfolds upon the Earth, and Satan and his forces gain strongholds seemingly everywhere, the scene now switches to Heaven. For millennia, the wicked one has had access to the very presence of God where he is constantly "standing... to resist" (Zechariah 3:1) the work of God. His most loathsome work is an attack against the saints of God for which he is called the "accuser of our brethren" (Revelation 12:10). There stands that dirty old lawyer again. There cries that vicious adversary. The oldest book

A SPIRITUAL STRUGGLE NEEDS SPIRITUAL WEAPONRY.

in the Bible, the book of Job, starts with his accusing the brethren. Ten chapters from the close of Scriptures, he is still at it.

The courage of Michael cannot be missed. The description of this foe would cause a lesser soldier to cower in fear, for he comes as a "great red dragon, having seven heads and ten horns" (Revelation 12:3). He is not coming as an "angel of light" (2 Corinthians 11:14) for this battle! There are no deceptions needed. As only he could, Charles Spurgeon described the enemy like this:

"Huge in bulk and terrible in appearance is this emblem of evil, and he is clothed with the horrible splendor peculiar to himself—the splendor of deadly hate and imperious rebellion. Bright and burning, like flames of fire, the huge serpent is terrible to gaze upon. The python is red with wrath and encrimsoned with persecuting malice."[1]

How tired Heaven must be of Satan! How the angels must groan when he makes his entrance! How the righteous in Heaven must join the saints on earth in crying, "…How long, O Lord, holy and true, dost thou not judge and avenge…" (Revelation 6:10)? How angelic forces of glory must yearn for the hour when they will engage this demon once and for all.

And that day is coming. Leading the troops will be none other than Michael himself. The evil one will cross the line for the final time, and the Father of Glory will nod to Michael and say, "He's all yours."

And a war will ensue that is beyond human comprehension.

When the smoke clears, there will be two definite results. First, Satan will be "cast out" (Revelation 12:9). He will not be ushered out. He will not be excused to leave. He will not be dismissed, but he will be thrown out. The second result goes like this, "...neither was their place found any more in heaven" (Revelation 12:8). Gone for good! Heaven is shouting, Hell is fuming, but the locks on the door have been changed. You have accused your last saint!

The Bible tells the struggling Christian to understand that the "...weapons of our warfare are not carnal..." (2 Corinthians 10:4). Our battle with "principalities" and "powers" cannot be fought with traditional weapons created by human hands, but a spiritual struggle needs spiritual weaponry. It will be unmistakably clear at the conflict in Heaven that fleshly armaments cannot conquer the dreadful one, and Michael will be ready to call on Heaven's finest arsenal. Amazingly, these arms are at the beck and call of God's people today. When they are brought forth, the enemy's knees begin to buckle; his body shakes in panic; and he has no answer. For all of his designs and devices, he never has nor ever will have a response against these weapons.

Michael "overcame" him. We can overcome him too.

SATAN FEARS THE BLOOD OF CHRIST

"...they overcame him by the blood of the Lamb..." (Revelation 12:10). Since the days of righteous Abel, Satan has waged his greatest onslaught against the blood of the Lamb. Sin "entered into the world" (Romans 5:12) creating havoc in the first family. Sin always presents a unique set of problems, not the least of which is finding a way to remove the guilt and trouble it creates.

Cain, Abel's brother, followed the natural religious instincts in the heart of a human, and brought "…of the fruit of the ground an offering unto the Lord" (Genesis 4:3). Certainly it was an expensive gift, a beautiful gift, and even a sincere gift, but a good work from human hands cannot buy forgiveness. Salvation is "Not by works of righteousness which we have done…" (Titus 3:5). With Cain's offering, man-made religion is born.

Abel offered "…unto God a more excellent sacrifice than Cain…" (Hebrews 11:4), a sacrifice though given thousands of years ago, preaches an emphatic message today. The sermon so resonates to the present day that God claimed, "…by it he being dead yet speaketh." It is transparent, unambiguous, and uncomplicated.

Would you be free from the burden of sin?

There is power in the Blood!

How the father of lies assaults the blood of the Lamb! Listen to the liberal ministers ascending powerless pulpits and mocking the "slaughterhouse religion"! Listen to the "progressive" professors in the hallowed halls of learning deriding the Cross! Listen to the "emerging church" experts trod "under foot the Son of God" and count His blood "an unholy thing" (Hebrews 10:29)!

Down the corridor of human history God reminded the righteous to focus on the blood of the Lamb. Moses not only told the Hebrews of impending judgment, but of salvation from the wrath of God. "…When I see the blood, I will pass over you…" (Exodus 12:13). When a sinner seeking forgiveness brought an animal to the altar, the priest was told to "bring the blood" (Leviticus 1:5). The blood painted a powerful picture of the appalling "wages of sin" (Romans 6:23). The blood reminded the comer that the innocent lamb had to be sacrificed to pay for the sins of the guilty. The blood prophesied of the coming day when God would send His Lamb, the Lamb that would take "away the sin of the world" (John 1:29).

The New Testament is replete with statements exalting the blood of Christ. Jesus said His blood was "shed for many for the remission of sins" (Matthew 26:28). He purchased His church "with his own blood" (Acts 20:28). If a sinner receives His forgiveness it is a result of "faith in his blood" (Romans 3:25). By His blood we are "justified" (Romans 5:9). By His blood "we have redemption" (Ephesians 1:7). By the blood of Christ we are "made nigh" (Ephesians 2:13). His blood purges our "conscience from dead works to serve the living God" (Hebrews 9:14), and it is by His blood that we have "boldness to enter into the holiest" (Hebrews 10:19). Throughout

ANY GOOD WORK FROM HUMAN HANDS NEVER HAS NOR EVER SHALL BUY FORGIVENESS.

eternity we will sing to the One who was slain, and "hast redeemed us to God by thy blood" (Revelation 5:9).

The righteous have always loved the blood of Christ! "He sought me and bought me with His redeeming blood!" Ask the man whose life was dominated by sin but has been set free, what he thinks of the blood. Ask the drunkard who took a swallow of the living water and now he never thirsts again! Ask the fornicator who was set free from the shackles of wickedness, the drug addict delivered from the needle, the sodomite, the thief, the extortioner. One by one, sinners down through the ages of time can testify as to what they used to be, but now they are "...washed...sanctified... [and] justified in the name of the Lord Jesus, and by the Spirit of our God" (1 Corinthians 6:11)! "...The blood of Jesus Christ his Son cleanseth us from all sin" (1 John 1:7)!

It is for good reason then that Satan so despises the royal blood of Christ. Watch him enter the golden portals of Heaven yet again to accuse the saints. See the smug, arrogant glare filling the face of this demonic prosecutor. Notice the brief he is carrying in his hands—another air-tight case against a hapless child of the King. "Here is the evidence! Here is the proof! It is undeniable!"

Now all eyes focus on the defense "advocate" (1 John 2:1). What hope could there be for such a sinner? What chance could prevail for a man as guilty as sin? Why, "...scarcely for a righteous man will one die...." Yes, "...for a good man some would even dare to die..." (Romans 5:7). But this is not a trial of a righteous man or even a good man. Standing ashamed is a helpless, powerless sinner who is "condemned already" (John 3:18). What will the "advocate" say?

The silence is deafening. All ears are waiting for a stinging rebuttal or a cutting cross examination, but the words never come. Instead, the "advocate" raises His hands toward the judge. Look at His hands! They are not just nail-scarred hands, they are wounded hands! Now comes the question on everyone's mind, "…What are these wounds in thine hands…?"

"…Those with which I was wounded in the house of my friends" (Zechariah 13:6).

Case closed!

"What about the fornicators and idolaters and adulterers and effeminate and abusers of themselves with mankind and thieves and covetous and drunkards and revilers and extortioners?" (1 Corinthians 6:9–10).

"Those, sir, are under the blood!"

"Surely you remember uncleaness, lasciviousness, idolatry, witchcraft, hatred, variance, emulations, wrath, strife, seditions, heresies, envyings, murders, drunkenness, revelings, and such like!" (Galatians 5:19–21).

"No sir, I remember them 'no more'" (Hebrews 10:17).

"What has then become of them?"

"All of those sins have been cast into 'the depths of the sea'" (Micah 7:19).

Hallelujah, what a Saviour!

"And they overcame him by the blood of the Lamb!" (Revelation 12:11).

The blood never fails for the child of God. It is true that the blood of Jesus washes our sins away so that we no longer fear death and Hell and eternity. But there is an immediate benefit as well. In the moment of temptation when the flesh and spirit are engaging the fight, we can trust Him. Cry out to the Saviour who cried from Calvary for you. Confess your own weakness and inability, and plead for His strength and His support. Desperate situations call for desperate pleading. He is an overcoming Saviour, and He will respond in time.

> THE BLOOD NEVER FAILS FOR THE CHILD OF GOD.

Have you been washed in the blood? Victory against Satan is only possible through the blood.

"And they overcame him by the blood of the Lamb!"

SATAN FEARS THE SURRENDERED LIFE

Theologians love to use profound words to describe the power of the blood of Christ, but the blood is effective in action. Dedicated saints who "loved not their lives unto the death" have invested their lives as a "word of their testimony" (Revelation 12:11). So grateful for the love of Christ at Calvary, they would join the Apostle Paul in saying, "For the love of Christ constraineth us….he died for all, that they which live should not henceforth live unto themselves, but unto him which died for them, and rose again" (2 Corinthians 5:14–15). Paul's own life was forever changed when he decided, "If Jesus can die for me, then I can live for Him."

The transformation of the disciples in the New Testament demonstrates the power of Calvary. Before Calvary, Jesus reminded them repeatedly that they were of "little faith" (Matthew 6:30). He asked them on a number of occasions questions such as, "...Are ye also yet without understanding" (Matthew 15:16)? In the Saviour's hour of greatest need they were first "sleeping for sorrow" (Luke 22:45), and ultimately they "forsook him, and fled" (Mark 14:50). Despite the bold promise of Peter, "...Though I should die with thee, yet will I not deny thee" (Matthew 26:35), it wasn't very long before he was cursing and denying Christ.

Then comes the book of Acts.

Watch Peter valiantly preach the risen Christ at Pentecost. Listen as Peter and John face the threats of the authorities with courage and conviction, so that their enemies had to take "knowledge of them" (Acts 4:13). Hear them boldly proclaim, "...Whether it be right in the sight of God to hearken unto you more than unto God, judge ye. For we cannot but speak the things which we have seen and heard" (Acts 4:19–20). They would be beaten, imprisoned, and finally martyred for their King.

John Foxe details their martyrdoms in the immortal *Book of Martyrs*.[2] Stephen, of course, was stoned; Pastor James was beheaded; and Matthew was murdered by a halberd in Africa. James had his brains beaten out; Matthias was stoned and then beheaded; and Andrew was crucified. Mark was dragged to his death; Peter was crucified upside down; and Paul "gave his neck to the sword." Jude, Simon, and Bartholomew were all crucified; Thomas was pierced through with a spear; and Doctor Luke was hanged on an olive tree. Only John was spared a violent death, yet he was cast into a cauldron of boiling oil and exiled to the island of criminals known as Patmos.

Their Saviour had paid the ultimate price for them, and they were finally ready to do "reasonable service" (Romans 12:1) for Him. They had sincerely thought they were ready to die for Him in the Gospels, but those earnest promises turned out to be hollow words. As the New Testament unfolds, Calvary's love changed everything. For John, it took a singular look at an empty sepulcher. For Thomas, it was a look at the pierced hands of Jesus. For Peter, it was the haunting question, "…lovest thou me more than these?" (John 21:15).

They truly "loved not their lives unto death," and the centuries that followed have only magnified the "word of their testimony." Satan had no answer for their courage. The driven nails of a cross could not stop them; the horrific beatings that slashed their flesh could not stop them; and the lonely nights in the depths of a brutal prison cell could not stop them. They had made their choice. They had sold out to Him. They had put it all on the altar of sacrifice and there was no turning back.

Jesus had told them, "…If any man will come after me, let him deny himself, and take up his cross, and follow me" (Matthew 16:24). And that is exactly what they had done. A man hanging on a cross cannot look behind him. A man hanging on a cross has no future. A man hanging on a cross can only look ahead. When these men took up their crosses for the One who went to the Cross for them, there would be no more profane denials, fearful flights, and sarcastic doubtings. It was full speed ahead, and this transmission had no reverse.

> THEIR SAVIOUR HAD PAID THE ULTIMATE PRICE FOR THEM, AND THEY WERE FINALLY READY TO DO "REASONABLE SERVICE."

They overcame him because they "loved not their lives unto death." Satan cannot deal with that. A man who decides, "For to me to live is Christ, and to die is gain" (Philippians 1:21) has been catapulted to the place of victory. When a man can say, "…I will not fear what man shall do unto me" (Hebrews 13:6), he has risen above the ordinary Christian, and is fighting a battle on grounds the devil cannot conquer.

In the 1950s, a veteran missionary in the land of India was told of a people in northeastern India known as the Garo tribe. He took the difficult journey, ultimately finding the tribe and a small but powerful little church in that village. He was immediately impressed by their dedication to Christ and willingness to pay the price for Him. He rejoiced in their music of praise and was encouraged by their faithful preaching.

When the pastor invited the missionary to a baptismal service, he was delighted. The small group of believers made their way to the riverside where a staggering scene began to unfold. As the candidates for baptism waded out into the river, the missionary noticed a crowd of villagers gathering on a nearby hillside, a crowd that soon was hostile towards the new converts. They would taunt and mock those standing for Christ. Some that were baptized would lose their jobs and others would be removed from their families. The entire town would know of their decision to be saved, and their desire to identify with Christ. Indeed, there was a cost to count for those who would follow the Saviour.

Then the missionary heard the church members sing a little chorus they had created for these baptisms, a little chorus they would sing to hearten people in making their choice for Christ. That little chorus, born in a poor, small Indian village, has made its way around the world encouraging saints to live for the One who is worthy. The words went like this:

> I have decided to follow Jesus. I have decided to follow
> Jesus. I have decided to follow Jesus.
> No turning back; no turning back.[3]

"And they overcame him by the blood of the Lamb, and by the word of their testimony; and they loved not their lives unto the death" (Revelation 12:11).

It is time to make our choice. It is time to take our stand. The saints of old have laid out the example of a surrendered life, but it is all in vain if we will not make our choice.

We must surrender our bodies to Him. "Lord, I give you my hands. Let them do as you wish. Lord, I give you my feet. Let them go where you wish. Lord, I give you my eyes. Let them see what you want them to see. Lord, I give you my ears. Let them hear what you desire."

We must surrender our priorities to Him. "Lord, I give you my family. I want to build my home on your Word. Lord, I give you my business. I want to exalt you in every area of my life. Lord, I give you my checkbook. I want to lay up treasures for eternity."

We must surrender our futures to Him. "Lord, I am willing to go where you would have me go, and to do with my life anything you wish." Nothing is held back. Nothing is left for future negotiations. It is all I have for Christ and all I am for Christ. Nothing less than complete sacrifice will make a man an overcomer.

Simply, there is a cost to being an overcomer. It will cost us everything. Will you pay that price?

"And they overcame him by the blood of the Lamb, and by the word of their testimony; and they loved not their lives unto the death."

CHAPTER SIX

THE ENEMY AND HIS FUTURE

The judgments that will fall upon the earth during the seven years of tribulation are humanly incomprehensible. When terrorists attacked the United States in 2001, the resulting panic and fear made that day of infamy a daily news story for years. As horrific as those events were for America, during the Tribulation, 9/11 will be considered a slow news day. News broadcasts will be full of wars, rumors of war, death, famine, havoc, celestial fireworks, destructive creatures, diseases, ravaging wild animals, and other assorted stories. The news channels will be in their glory. "Breaking news" will be the norm.

The book of Revelation divides these events into a series of judgments which are triggered in Revelation 6. One by one, seven seals are broken open revealing the wrath of God upon the wickedness of men. The seventh seal leads to the sounding of seven trumpets which ushers in the judgments of the seven vials. Each of these twenty-one judgments reveals the holy rage of God relentlessly cascading on a deserving world. The eminent king, the opulent millionaire, the robust soldier, the potent athlete, and the penniless pauper will face the same fate. The floods of fear will overwhelm them to the place where they will run to the caves and beg them to "...Fall on us, and hide us from the face of him that sitteth on the throne, and from the wrath of the Lamb" (Revelation 6:16).

One of the amazing aspects of human nature is the unwillingness of a man to humble himself before God. It would be natural to assume that the time of unparalleled trouble would produce a contrite spirit, but the Bible says differently. When half of the world population is dead, and those who remain are suffering incredible torment, the Bible explains human reaction like this: "...the rest of the men which were not killed by these plagues yet repented not of the works of their hands..." (Revelation 9:20).

The God who "...knoweth the secrets of the heart" (Psalm 44:21) explains mortal reasoning. Bible repentance requires a choice. Will a man choose the God of the Bible or the "works of their hands"? Will he choose the God of the Bible or "devils"? Will he choose the God of the Bible or "idols of gold, and silver, and brass, and stone, and of wood"? Will he choose the God of the Bible or his murders, sorceries, fornication, and thefts (Revelation 9:20–21)? Sadly, men would rather suffer than choose Christ.

Yet even more astounding will be the vitriol and venom sinners will heap upon the righteous. A legion of people will respond to the Gospel in these darkest of days and trust Christ. They will be the focus of Satan and his forces. They will be blamed for world events and become the latest group of persecuted saints "…slain for the word of God, and for the testimony which they held" (Revelation 6:9).

From the depths of these saints will emerge this cry, "…How long, O Lord, holy and true, dost thou not judge and avenge our blood" (Revelation 6:10)? That plea echoes down the corridor of human history. When righteous people watch their lives crumble, when the physical torture is unbearable, when

BIBLE REPENTANCE REQUIRES A CHOICE.

sorrow overwhelms them, and when anguish swells over their souls, there are no pills or programs or proverbs that can stem the flood. Sometimes there are no explanations. Sometimes there are no answers. Sometimes there is only one thing to cry.

"How long, O Lord?"

Throughout the corridor of Scriptures, this wail of the righteous has winged its way to Heaven. "How long?" Hear patient Job in his hour of heartbreak wailing over his lost loved ones. His wife had turned bitter toward God and his own flesh was rotting before his very eyes. His familiars have come pontificating with lengthy displays of human wisdom that miss the mark every time. Hear him come to the end of the road and cry, "How long will ye vex my soul, and break me in pieces with words" (Job 19:2)?

Listen as David faces the chastening hand of the hot displeasure of God's wrath. His family is crumbling, his kingdom is collapsing, his health is decaying, and he is emotionally consumed. His bones were "vexed," his soul was "sore vexed," his tears filled his bed, and "grief" dominated his life. He could do one thing. He could lift up his soul to Heaven and cry, "How long?" (Psalm 6).

Watch as the prophet Isaiah is commissioned by Heaven. He sees a vision of the holiness of God that drives him to his knees. His own pitiful condition only magnifies the compassion of God's merciful forgiveness, and then comes the question of the ages. "...Whom shall I send, and who will go for us...?" An incredulous Isaiah can only volunteer. "...Here am I; send me" (Isaiah 6:8).

THE HUMAN HEART HAS OFTEN TURNED TO HEAVEN ASKING, "HOW LONG?"

Perhaps visions of ministry fill the thinking of Isaiah. "Will I preach like the prophet Elijah? Will I part the seas like our father Moses? Will I pen resplendent songs like the man after God's own heart? Will I move Heaven with prayer as did the priestly Samuel?" God had something else in mind.

He told Isaiah that he would preach to a crowd that would hear and not understand; they would see and yet not get it. His duty was to "Make the heart of this people fat, and make their ears heavy, and shut their eyes…" (Isaiah 6:10). Not exactly the message one expects at his ordination.

See a confused preacher look to Heaven and ask the simple question, "…How long…" (Isaiah 6:11)?

Watch the tears streaming down the face of the weeping prophet Jeremiah. His family and friends had long since abandoned him. He knew the disgust of Jerusalem's prison system, and had faced the ridicule of spending a day locked in the stocks by the gate. He was the object of scorn as the ministers heaped their contempt on him, and even the king despised him. He watched his nation reject the Word of God, the standards of God, and the love of God. He was allowed to see the impending doom of God that was ready to fall upon the city he loved, and Jeremiah could only cry, "How long shall the land mourn?" (Jeremiah 12:4).

Hear the gallant Habakkuk as he watches violence, iniquity, robbery, and fighting fill the streets. The courts protect the criminals and punish the righteous. Wrong had become right and right had become wrong. Everything was backwards, and God's man expected God to intervene. "…How long shall I cry and thou will not hear! Even cry out unto thee of violence, and thou will not save" (Habakkuk 1:2)!

"How long, O Lord?"

Indeed, those tribulation saints will be in good company.

The human heart has often turned to Heaven asking, "How long?" How long will wicked governments murder and torture people? How long will evil religions mock the grace of God? How long will depraved individuals get away with their crimes? We see assaults on children go unpunished. We see corruption in our officials ignored. We see governors condone Sodomite marriages and condemn homeschooling mothers. We want to cry with David, "It is time for thee, Lord, to work…" (Psalm 119:126).

We see sweet, godly saints suffering on beds of affliction waiting to go home to Heaven. We feel the heartbreak of the newly married wife burying her soldier husband. We gaze into the eyes of little children lying in a hospital room as a dread disease sucks their lives away and nothing can be done.

And we cry out, "How long, O Lord?" It seems to be the question without an answer.

But there is an answer. "How long, O Lord?" "Until Revelation 19!"

As the insurmountable tidal wave of Tribulation engulfs the earth, Pastor John gazes in amazement as the final chapter unfolds. Imagine the tribulation saint who has dodged the executioner. He has seen the world masses follow Satan's emissary. He has watched the economies of the world collapse into worthlessness. Death and carnage by every means imaginable, and some means the science fiction fan would never believe, have filled the earth with blood.

Earthquakes around the globe have shaken capitols and villages, and fireworks in the heavens have fallen to the earth with cataclysmic results. Chaos abounds as "Men's hearts failing them for fear…" (Luke 21:26) leave a path of death and darkness.

A man looks to the government but finds no help. He looks to his wealth but it has disappeared. He looks to his own human strength and finds it has abandoned him. The earth is teetering on the brink of annihilation. When there is no place else to look, the stage has finally been properly prepared. The preliminaries are now officially out of the way and history's climax will unfold.

"Behold, he cometh with clouds; and every eye shall see him…" (Revelation 1:7). "…Behold, the Lord cometh with ten thousands of his saints" (Jude 14). "When the Son of man shall come in his glory…" (Matthew 25:31). "Then shall the Lord go forth…" (Zechariah 14:3). "…Surely I come quickly" (Revelation 22:20). "…I will come again…" (John 14:3).

> Lift up your heads, pilgrims aweary,
> See day's approach now crimson the sky;
> Night shadows flee, and your Beloved,
> Awaited with longing, at last draweth nigh.
> He is coming again, He is coming again,
> The very same Jesus, rejected of men;
> He is coming again, He is coming again,
> With power and great glory, He is coming again![1]

It will be the singular event of the ages, and Pastor John has already seen it!

"And I saw Heaven opened, and behold a white horse; and he that sat upon him was called Faithful and True…." His eyes are as a "flame of fire." His head holds "many crowns." His title was unrecognizable. His clothing was "dipped in blood." His name is the "Word of God." From His mouth comes a "sharp sword." And on His thigh is the name that says it all: "…KING OF KINGS, AND LORD OF LORDS" (Revelation 19:11–16).

Envision the response of the human. There stands the religious man who has only heard of the religious Christ. He pictures a tall, soft-spoken, kindly man with flowing long hair. On the wall of his home hang pictures of Jesus holding little lambs, or quietly knocking on the door, or bowing reverently in prayer. His favorite religious charm is a golden cross he wears around his neck. His minister never preached about the wrath of Christ. His Sunday school teacher never told him of the holiness of Christ. His favorite TV minister never cared enough to warn him about the consequences of sin.

Now he sees the Christ of glory and power instantly vanquishing the world and its religions. Too late he realizes that the Christ of religion and the Christ of the Bible are very different individuals. Too late he realizes his mild, reserved Christ is actually one whose voice is as the "sound of many waters." Too late he discerns his long-haired Christ instead has hair that is pure and "white like wool." Too late is his discovery that his good-luck Christ in truth radiates with holiness "as the sun shineth in his strength" (Revelation 1:14–16).

"And when I saw him, I fell at his feet as dead" (Revelation 1:17).

There stands the liberal seminary professor. His favorite hobby was dissecting the Bible, and he called himself a "higher critic." Hear him sneer at the Creationist. Listen to him scoff at Noah and his ark. Watch him postulate his theories contradicting every clear doctrine in the Bible. He denies the miracles of the Bible, the Christ of the Bible, and the salvation of the Bible. He is an enemy of God's written Word.

> THE COMING KING WILL TURN DESPAIR INTO HOPE, DEFEAT INTO VICTORY, AND DEATH INTO LIFE.

Now he sees the Heavens open. The Christ he claimed was dead is very much alive. The Bible he corrected is now unfolding literally before his eyes. When he sees the glorious Christ, he will discover that "…his name is called Word of God" (Revelation 19:13). Too late he realizes that his feeble, foul, loathsome assaults against the written Words of God were, in truth, onslaughts against the omnipotent living Word of God. The one he had "trodden under foot" (Hebrews 10:29) hour after hour is the same Jesus filling the skies as the lightning coming out of the east and shining "unto the west" (Matthew 24:27).

"And when I saw him, I fell at his feet as dead!"

Watch the blasphemer who only knew the name of Christ as a curse word. He never found time to open the Bible and read that His name is "above every name" (Philippians 2:9). He cares not that God told Joseph, "…thou shalt call his name JESUS: for he shall save his people from their sins" (Matthew 1:21). He is not impressed that the holy Son of God is above "every name that is named, not only in this world, but also in that which is to come" (Ephesians 1:21). He callously drags the name of the God of the Bible and His precious Son through the mud. As it was in the days of Isaiah, truly it is with him: "…my name continually every day is blasphemed" (Isaiah 52:5).

Now the One he mocked and cursed and profaned is coming in righteousness to "judge and make war." The man whose jagged tongue would take the name of Christ in vain will not escape the fact that "out of his mouth goeth a sharp sword" (Revelation 19:11). The tongue that swore against the pure Son of God will now have to face His mouth and His words and His sword. Knees begin to buckle and strength disappears. "…at the name of Jesus every knee should bow…and every tongue…confess that Jesus Christ is Lord, to the glory of God the Father" (Philippians 2:10–11).

"And when I saw him, I fell at his feet as dead!"

"How long, O Lord?"

As the King of kings and Lord of lords descends in glory, the Antichrist and his armies will amass for the battle of the ages. It will be over before it begins. This battle will not employ the latest military hardware. This battle will not engage the finest fighting machines, nor will it need a nuclear device. The conquering Christ speaks the Word, and John describes the end of Satan's emissaries.

"And the beast was taken, and with him the false prophet that wrought miracles before him, with which he deceived them that had received the mark of the beast, and them that worshiped his image. These both were cast alive into a lake of fire burning with brimstone" (Revelation 19:20).

It will be a glorious day when the evil antichrist and his abominable religious hierarchy are forever vanquished. To the tribulation saints, those seven years will certainly seem like seven decades. Yet, the coming King will turn despair into hope, defeat into victory, and death into life. "...even so, come, Lord Jesus" (Revelation 22:20)!

But there is one more task on the agenda. John saw it all happen in Revelation 20:1–3:

> "And I saw an angel come down from heaven, having the key of the bottomless pit and a great chain in his hand. And he laid hold on the dragon, that old serpent, which is the Devil, and Satan, and bound him a thousand years, and cast him into the bottomless pit, and shut him up, and set a seal upon him, that he should deceive the nations no more, till the thousand years should be fulfilled: and after that he must be loosed a little season."

The Bible experts have surmised as to who this unidentified angel is. The esteemed commentator Matthew Henry believed it will be Jesus Himself. "He is one who has power to bind the strong man armed, to cast him out, and to spoil his goods; and therefore must be stronger than he."[2] His dominant coming will set off a series of ironies that will delight those who carry the battle scars from their bouts with the enemy.

The angel comes with a key. The last time the key was mentioned in the Bible it was in the paws of the grimy, evil one. He opened a "bottomless pit" in Revelation 9:2 inflicting horrific torture on humanity. This time, however, the key no longer is under the control of the dragon but rather safely in the hands of the Heavenly emissary. Satan will be left "keyless."

JESUS COULD NOT BE SEALED! THE GRAVE COULD NOT CONTAIN HIM!

He comes carrying a great chain as well. How fitting that this enemy who has chained multitudes with his own devices is about ready to get his "comeuppance." The "chainer" is about ready to become the "chainee."

The God of the Bible makes sure the identity of the wicked one. This same lawyer that would stand at the bar of Heaven and identify the names of the brethren will finally hear his name called. There will be no mistake. One may call him the dragon, one may call him the serpent, one may call him the devil, one may call him

Satan, but when Jesus is through with him, we will just call him history. The "name-caller" will hear his name echo through the judgment halls.

The angel will cast the wicked one into a bottomless pit, which will be a one thousand year abode for him. In the book of Revelation, Satan often uses that pit to create havoc on the earth. Now, he will be hurled into this penitentiary, and there will be no escape. The Bible says he will be "shut...up" (what a choice of words in our English Bible) and sealed. Glory!

When Jesus gave His life on the Cross, the religious foes gathered themselves to Pilate. Their request was that Pilate command the authorities to make the tomb secure. No disciple would steal His body and claim a resurrection. Pilate said, "...Ye have a watch: go your way, make it as sure as ye can. So they went, and made the sepulcher sure, sealing the stone and setting a watch" (Matthew 27:65–66).

See Satan and his servants shout in triumph as the stone is set. The Messiah was dead and buried and the grave was secure. Roman sentinels would take four hour shifts through the night surveying that gravesite making it so.

How foolish to think that a human seal could stop the "Resurrection and the life" (John 11:25)! As the angel of the Lord descended in the midst of a thundering earthquake, Jesus rose again! He could not be sealed! The grave could not contain Him!

"…thanks be to God, which giveth us the victory through our Lord Jesus Christ" (1 Corinthians 15:57)!

One day the "sealer" will become the "sealee"! Evangelist Gary Gillmore would often say, "I hope when they put him in the pit, the Lord lets me jump up and down a few times on the lid to make sure it is shut!"

Charles Spurgeon put it like this:

> "We can see the heel mark of Christ upon his broken head, and what is more we expect to set our own heel there, for we are told that the Lord will bruise Satan under our foot shortly. I reckon upon the time when the Lord will bruise him under my foot, it shall be as heavy a bruise as I can give him, I warrant you."[3]

For one thousand years Jesus will rule the world in peace. "And he shall judge among many people, and rebuke strong nations afar off; and they shall beat their swords into plowshares, and their spears into pruning hooks: nation shall not lift up a sword against nation, neither shall they learn war any more" (Micah 4:3). "The wolf also shall dwell with the lamb, and the leopard shall lie down with the kid; and the calf and the young lion and the fatling together; and a little child shall lead them" (Isaiah 11:6). "And the LORD shall be king over all the earth: in that day shall there be one LORD, and his name one" (Zechariah 14:9).

The Saviour is not quite finished with Satan yet. "And when the thousand years are expired, Satan shall be loosed out of his prison, and shall go out to deceive the nations…" (Revelation 20:7–8). As incredible as it seems, even during the one thousand year reign of Christ, countless numbers, "the number of whom is as the sand of the sea," will garner resentment and rebellion toward Christ. Like many religious people of today, they will honor Him with their lips but their hearts will be elsewhere. Indeed, "The heart is deceitful above all things and desperately wicked…" (Jeremiah 17:9).

The Dragon will be released from his holding cell and explode upon the world with his pent up wrath and fury. He will gather his crowd for one final attempt to battle the Messiah. He has fought Him every step of the way. From the Garden of Eden, to the Royal line of the Old Testament, to the Manger in Bethlehem, to the Garden of Gethsemane, to the Cross of Calvary, to the Tomb of Joseph, and to the Plains of Megiddo, Satan has relentlessly brandished his sword against the "Lion of the tribe of Judah" (Revelation 5:5). This will be his final battle.

As his armies surround Jerusalem, "fire came down from God out of heaven, and devoured them." Adios. Before he knows what hit him, he will be tossed into the eternal "lake of fire and brimstone." He will be with his buddies from the Tribulation known as the "beast and the false prophet." And He "shall be tormented day and night forever and ever"! What a day that will be (Revelation 20:9–10)!

"How long, O Lord?"

It may be at morn, when the day is awaking,

When sunlight through darkness and shadow is breaking

That Jesus will come in the fullness of glory

To receive from the world "His own."

It may be at midday, it may be at twilight,

It may be, perchance, that the blackness of midnight

Will burst into light in the blaze of His glory,

When Jesus receives "His own."

While its hosts cry Hosanna, from heaven descending,

With glorified saints and the angels attending,

With grace on His brow, like a halo of glory,

Will Jesus receive "His own."

Oh, joy! oh, delight! should we go without dying,

No sickness, no sadness, no dread and no crying.

Caught up through the clouds with our Lord into glory,

When Jesus receives "His own."

O Lord Jesus, how long, how long

Ere we shout the glad song,

Christ returneth! Hallelujah!

Hallelujah! Amen. Hallelujah! Amen.[4]

June 25, 2005, was a clear night in the mountains of Afghanistan.[5] Marcus Luttrell and three other Navy SEALs landed in the rugged terrain with the mission of capturing or killing the notorious Taliban commander, Ben Sharmak. Sharmak's bloodthirsty command included some two hundred soldiers who at his leadership represented terrorists at their worst. It was in these mountains that Osama Bin Laden and people like Ben Sharmak had planned their demonic attacks against New York City.

Within a few days, the Navy SEALS would suffer the largest loss of life in their illustrious history. The men were trapped by the Taliban on a steep mountain leading to a vicious fire fight. The Taliban fighters had the advantage with the higher ground, causing the Americans to scramble down the mountainside to seek an advantage. They literally fell headlong downward grabbing any tree or rock that would slow their descent.

Their situation worsened. One of the men's hands was blown apart but he refused to quit. They desperately sought a foothold but found none. Though they had killed scores of the enemy, replacements with a bounty of ammunition were right behind them. A ninety minute battle resulted in the death of three brave SEALs leaving Marcus Luttrell as the lone survivor, yet he knew he was not alone. He wrote his story with these words, "I had only one Teammate. And He moved, as ever, in mysterious ways. But I was a Christian, and He had somehow saved me from a thousand AK-47 bullets on this day. No one had shot me, which was well nigh beyond all comprehension." 6

The American command sent a helicopter with sixteen soldiers to fight the battle. From a Taliban bunker a rocket-propelled grenade was fired at the fuel tanks bringing them down. In the violent crash, each of the men was killed.

Luttrell tried to escape with his life. By now he was badly wounded, bleeding, and choking with thirst, but he pressed on. A desperate feeling of desolation nearly overcame him but he kept moving. Frequently he fell down the mountainside, but he survived the night.

The next morning, Luttrell was shot in the thigh by a Taliban sniper. With more bullets ricocheting around the granite mountain, the wounded American hero was reduced to crawling on all fours. Eventually he came upon a small pool of water. Luttrell dove in the water drinking and washing his wounds. When he looked up, he was staring at three Afghans holding weapons. They began shouting at him.

Incredibly, the Afghanis did not finish him off. He soon realized they wanted to help him and they risked their lives hiding him in their village known as Sabray for the next five days. He would move from huts to caves sleeping on rooftops, and running from the eyes of the Taliban. Luttrell's time would be limited for he was discovered by the Taliban, meaning the inevitable battle would have to be fought. He knew he had to leave the village.

During the week, Luttrell lost thirty-seven pounds. His face was scoured, his nose was broken, his thigh was wounded from the shot, two bones were broken in his wrist, three vertebrae were cracked, and he had lost an incredible amount of blood. Yet he had to go on the run again. The brave villagers who had risked their lives for him could not be placed in greater danger. Sharmak had told the village chief that if Luttrell was not released, the chief's family would be killed.

Once again, he found himself in the jagged mountains encircled by the Taliban. His perilous hiding place would not hold for long. It appeared the week long struggle for life was coming to a tragic end. He was surrounded and all hope was gone. Here is how he described it:

> And here I was, alone with these tribesmen, with no coherent plan. My leg was killing me, I could hardly put it to the ground, and the two guys carrying me were bearing the whole of my weight. We came to a little flight of rough rock steps cut into the gradient. They got behind pushing me up with their shoulders.
>
> I made the top step first, and as I did so, I came face to face with an armed Afghani fighter I had not seen before. He carried an AK-47, held it in the ready-to-fire position, and when he saw me he raised it. I looked at his hat, and there was a badge containing the words which almost stopped my heart—BUSH FOR PRESIDENT. [7]

Luttrell realized the man was Afghan Special Forces. Right behind were two U.S. Army Rangers in combat uniforms. When he lifted up his eyes, "Army guys were coming out of the forest from all over the place." One of the Rangers asked the question, "American?" Marcus Luttrell was rescued.

This story is but a shadow of the rescue of the tribulation saints. The earth will be saddled with "distress of nations, with perplexity; the sea and the waves roaring; men's hearts failing them for fear." The "signs in the sun and in the moon and in the stars" will cause the "powers of heaven" to be "shaken." Human life will literally be on the verge of annihilation when suddenly, all eyes will turn Heavenward.

"And then shall they see the Son of man coming in a cloud with power and great glory!"

Jesus told His persecuted people what to do next. "Look up, and lift up your heads; for your redemption draweth nigh" (Luke 21:25–28)!

God's people will finally be rescued from the roaring lion. We will finally get our answer to "How long, O Lord?"

CHAPTER SEVEN

THE ENEMY'S DESIRE FOR YOU

It was the night before the Cross. No one would have blamed Christ for putting His own needs first, but His habit was to be "moved with compassion" (Matthew 9:36). Even as He hung on the Cross hours later with nails piercing His hands and feet, with the thorns crushed into His brow, with His life's blood spewing from His mangled flesh, and the spittle of the soldiers streaming down His face, He could only see others. He took care of His mother. He took care of His enemies asking His Father to "forgive them; for they know not what they do" (Luke 23:34). He found time to save a destitute criminal, and, of course, He took extreme care to be certain "that the scripture should be fulfilled" (John 19:36). What an amazing Saviour.

It should not be surprising then to glean Christ's grave concern for Peter. In Luke 22:31 He calls him, "Simon, Simon." That should have immediately arrested Peter's attention for two reasons. In Bible times, when a name was repeated, it was always an expression of deep compassion combined with warning.[1] Even more alarming, was the fact that Jesus used the 'old' name Simon, not the 'new' name Peter. Looking back it becomes easy to discern the message that Peter was about to revert to the ways of the old man despite his claim that he was ready to go to "prison and to death."

Satan, the great adversary, was poised to strike. His main target was, of course, the Son of God, but Peter was in the cross-hairs as well. Jesus put it like this, "Satan hath desired to have you, that he may sift you as wheat." The devil wanted to reclaim Peter as his own. It is the only occasion that this particular word "sift" is found in the New Testament, yet it shows the wicked one's purpose. He wanted Peter back.[2] He wanted to "sift" him "as wheat."

He wants to sift you until your life is ruined, your marriage is shattered, your family is decimated, and hope is gone. He wants your children, he wants your church, he wants your morals, he wants your spirit, he wants your body, and he wants any thing else he can get his grimy hands on.

Christ wants you as well. That is the reason He told Peter, "...I have prayed for thee, that thy faith fail not..." (Luke 22:32). Knowing the impact the Cross and the empty tomb would have on

Peter, He promised that one day He would strengthen Peter, and Peter in turn would "strengthen thy brethren."

A man who triumphs in the battle becomes a stronger man. There may be scars, even permanent scars from the battle, but when we grasp the truth that victory waits for the man who obediently trusts Christ, the culmination is a solid Christian soldier. The result of every conquest is a stronger man, a stronger family, a stronger church, stronger convictions, and a man reinforced for tomorrow's skirmish.

Don't quit the battle. Don't be weary in the trenches. Don't be discouraged by temporary setbacks. Jesus is still on the throne!

The enemy wants you.

The Saviour wants you.

You make the final choice.

APPENDIX

WHAT WILL YOU DO
WITH CHRIST?

ontrary to the human presumption that we are 'all the
sons of God', the Bible paints a different picture. In truth,
we are born into Satan's family. David could say, "...in
sin did my mother conceive me" (Psalm 51:5). As Jesus told the
religious crowd the message stands today, "Ye are of your father the
devil..." (John 8:44). The Bible states, "He that committeth sin is of
the devil..." (1 John 3:8). By nature, we are not the children of God
but rather "children of wrath" (Ephesians 2:3). The reason a man
needs to be "born again" (John 3:7) is because he was born into the
wrong family the first time.

The great dragon is interested in keeping his family together.
He is interested in populating the Hell that was "prepared for the
devil and his angels" (Matthew 25:41). Therein lies the battle for your

soul. On one side of the battlefield Satan and his cohorts wage war for your eternity. Standing in opposition is the Christ of the Bible who died "for our sins" (1 Corinthians 15:3). The greatest choice a man will make was voiced by Pilate, "…What shall I do then with Jesus which is called Christ" (Matthew 27:22)?

There can be no straddling of the fence. You must decide one way or the other. "He that is not with me is against me…" (Luke 11:23). You will either trust Him as "the way, the truth, and the life" (John 14:6), or you will try to climb to Heaven "some other way" (John 10:1). God's plan of salvation is simple because it is singular. Jesus is not a part of salvation, He is salvation. Jesus does not help you get to Heaven, He is your only hope of Heaven. When it comes to eternal life, there is one way and no other way. "Neither is there salvation in any other: for there is none other name under heaven given among men, whereby we must be saved" (Acts 4:12).

The plea of the Bible could not be more clear. "That if thou shalt confess with thy mouth the Lord Jesus, and shalt believe in thine heart that God hath raised him from the dead, thou shalt be saved. For with the heart man believeth unto righteousness; and with the mouth confession is made unto salvation" (Romans 10:9–10).

My reader friend, I plead with you to trust Jesus to wash your sins away. I implore you to "Search the scriptures…" (John 5:39). Be sure your eternity is settled by the words of God—not the words of religion. Be certain you are trusting the Christ of the Bible.

The ultimate enemy is after your eternal soul. What will you do with Christ?

CHAPTER ONE

1   Peter Capstick, *Death in the Long Grass* (New York: St. Martin's Press, 1977).

2   Spiros Zodhiates, *The Complete Word Study Dictionary* (Chattanooga: AMG International, Inc., 1993).

3   Capstick.

CHAPTER TWO

1   ESPN.com, "Specter Irked by Uncooperative Pats," February 22, 2008.

2   BIOPROJ.Sabr.com, Marge Schott, March, 1991.

3   Marvin Vincent, *Vincent's Word Studies* (McLean, VA: MacDonald Publishers), 198.

4   John Phillips, *Exploring Matthew* (Grand Rapids: Kregel, 2005).

5   Scripps Howard News Service, "Too May Americans Abuse Prescription Drugs," March 12, 2008.

6   Robert Morgan, *Then Sings My Soul* (Nashville: Thomas Nelson, 2003), 280.

7   Spiros Zodhiates, *The Complete Word Study Dictionary* (Chattanooga: AMG International, Inc., 1993).

8   Ibid.

9   NewsMax.com, "Bible Stopped Sniper's Bullet," August 9, 2007.

Chapter Three

1   *The New Brown-Driver-Briggs Gesenius Hebrew and English Lexicon*, (Peabody, MA: Hendrickson, 1979).

2   John Phillips, *Exploring Psalms* (Grand Rapids: Kregel, 2002), 293.

3   John Gill, *John Gill's Exposition of the Entire Bible*, Notes on Psalm 38.

4   Zodhiates.

5   2000+ Bible Illustrations, Module available on ESword Bible Program.

CHAPTER FOUR

1 Spiros Zodhiates, *The Complete Word Study Dictionary* (Chattanooga: AMG International, Inc., 1993).

2 P. L. Tan, *Encyclopedia of 7700 illustrations: A treasury of illustrations, anecdotes, facts and quotations for pastors, teachers and Christian workers,* Entry #6607, (Bible Communications: Garland TX, 1996, c1979).

3 E. D. Radmacher, R. B. Allen, & H. W. House, *Nelson's New Illustrated Bible Commentary* (T. Nelson Publishers: Nashville, 1999).

CHAPTER FIVE

1 Charles Spurgeon, *How They Conquered the Dragon*, Message preached May 30, 1875.

2 John Foxe, *Foxe's Book of Martyrs* (Grand Rapids, MI: Baker, 1978).

3 William Reynolds, *Songs of Glory* (Grand Rapids, MI: Baker, 1990).

CHAPTER SIX

1 Mabel Camp, *He is Coming Again* 1918.

2   Matthew Henry, *Commentary on the Whole Bible* (Hendrickson Pub).

3   Charles Spurgeon, *How They Conquered the Dragon*, Preached May 30, 1875.

4   H.L. Turner, *Christ Returneth* 1878.

5   Marcus Luttrell, *Lone Survivor* (New York: Little and Brown, 2007).

6   Ibid., 244.

7   Ibid., 348.

CHAPTER SEVEN

1   Adam Clarke, *Adam Clarke's Commentary on the Bible* (Thomas Nelson Incorporated, 1996).

2   Spiros Zodhiates, *The Complete Word Study Dictionary* (Chattanooga: AMG International, Inc., 1993).

Visit us online

strivingtogether.com

wcbc.edu